MW00562927

From Bluegrass to Blue Water

LESSONS IN FARM PHILOSOPHY AND NAVY LEADERSHIP

To Clara,
It is a real pleasure signing out this book to a fellow Kentuckian. Keep the faith!
John Palmer

John Palmer

Rear Admiral, U.S. Navy, Retired

FIDELIS PUBLISHING®

ISBN: 9781956454154
ISBN (eBook): 9781956454161

From Bluegrass to Blue Water:
Lessons in Farm Philosophy and Navy Leadership

Cover Design by Diana Lawrence
Interior Design by Xcel Graphic
Edited by Amanda Varian

Fidelis Publishing, LLC Sterling, VA • Nashville, TN
www.fidelispublishing.com

Manufactured in the United States of America
10 9 8 7 6 5 4 3 2 1

I dedicate this book to my wife, Brooks, and our children:
Elizabeth and John Taylor

Brooks and the kids in Mayport, Florida, in 1995

ACKNOWLEDGMENTS

This is a book of lessons. Despite my efforts, some of the lessons outlined were not always well executed on my part. I did not strike the balance between work and home life as well as I should. It is for that reason the most fitting dedication I can make is to my wife, Brooks, and our children: Elizabeth and John Taylor. In my naval career of thirty-two years, we made nineteen moves and lived in twelve states. My wife and I married in my first year of service, so she made the long hard slog. Our kids were kites dancing in the hurricane of military life for their first eighteen years. In one six-year period we moved five times from as far east as Chesapeake Bay, Maryland, to as far west as Oahu, Hawaii.

On one move, we raced cross-country in just a few days but still missed an opportunity to secure the military housing of our choice, so our daughter attended three separate kindergartens in that school year in Florida and California. Our son attended three separate middle schools over three years in the states of Virginia, Maryland, and Pennsylvania. My wife endured four ship tours totaling almost nine years on sea duty with much of that time apart. She kissed away tears, struck some form of normalcy, and kept the home fires burning for her Sailor-husband. Brooks managed two pairs of aging parents who are no longer with us, and she hurdled life-threatening medical issues alone.

Even when assigned ashore, an average day for me was eleven hours of work or more. She managed the family, completed nursing school, and became a registered nurse spending most of her career in hospital emergency departments. By my calculation, Brooks lost $30,000 in earning power with every move from stopping work, executing the move, getting relicensed in a new state, searching for a job, going through indoctrination, break-in periods, and finally being trusted as a new RN. My wife and kids were always the newbies at work and school.

Still, we moved, leaned on each other, survived, and often thrived. Our kids were blessed with good public schools wherever we were stationed. They navigated high school and graduated college on time—in good fashion. They both found wonderful mates, have impressive careers, and they have blessed Brooks and me with four incredible grandchildren.

As stated, I could have done better in balancing the scales for my family, but sometimes I did not. I have in speeches credited my wife with holding the family together while simultaneously "rescuing me from me"—or keeping my farm kid mischievousness in check. So, if anyone deserves recognition for enabling my career success, it is my tireless wife Brooks and our two phenomenal adult children who represent our pride and joy. In addition, Brooks and I delight in being "Lolli and Pop" to our four grandchildren as they are new blessings on top of lives already richly blessed. To my family goes my thanks, my respect, and my love.

In addition to my Navy family, my extended family was integral to this book, both in life experiences and the review process. My earliest influences were obviously my parents, the late Howard Hill Palmer and Mary Taylor Palmer. Thanks, Mom and Dad! In addition to the wonderful lessons and inspiration provided by my family, my wife (Brooks Mahaffey Palmer), daughter (Elizabeth Palmer Sanders), son (John Taylor Palmer Jr.), brother (Colonel Samuel Palmer U.S. Army [retired]), sister (Susan Palmer McVey), and cousin and best man (James Mitchell Burd, Esq.) read and provided recommendations for accuracy and revision. Jim Burd also provided deft legal advice as he has done so many times in the past.

I was guided by several long-term friends who are published authors, and they offered critical expertise and advice on the manuscript and processes for publication. These friends include Briar Hill

Elementary School classmate Robert C. Hall (Nathaniel Sewell), Citadel classmate Thomas L "Roy" Jeffords '88, Professor Bruce Craven of Columbia University, and Rear Admiral James McNeal U.S. Navy (retired)—serving currently as adjunct professor at his alma mater (United States Naval Academy). Professor Craven also introduced me to author, Therese Allison, who contributed insightful recommendations as I began to engage industry experts. I interviewed over a dozen publicists for potential service, and they referred me to fellow cohorts as well as contacts in publishing houses. These publicists are too numerous to mention here; however, they helped me accrue a valuable baseline of knowledge to advance the book within the industry—thank you.

Of special note, publicist Jason Jones of Jones Literary referred me to Gary Terashita, chief operating officer of Fidelis Publishing—both located in Nashville, Tennessee. Fidelis is a faith-infused organization with whom I am proud to be associated. My deepest appreciation to Gary and the team at Fidelis for making this book possible.

Finally, I would be remiss if I did not acknowledge the outstanding military and civil-servant mentors, peers, and especially those in support throughout my naval career. These include unit commanding officers, deputies, executive directors, executive officers, chiefs of staff, offices-in-charge, aides de camp, staff assistants, senior enlisted leaders from the chief petty officers' mess, administrative and secretarial staff, and always—always the enlisted *bluejacket Sailors* and *devil-dog Marines* with whom I have deployed and in whom our freedoms are entrusted.

Many thanks to all and keep charging!
JTP

CONTENTS

INTRODUCTION

The lessons contained within this book are derived from firsthand experience only, as I believe experience is the best teacher. No science, survey, or independent research is involved although a few famous phrases or summarizations from books, the Bible, and other leaders will be highlighted.

My siblings and I shared a childhood in a home with two loving parents emphasizing equal parts faith, farm, and education. We attended college paid partly by our parents as well as self-funding and scholarships. We graduated from colleges far away from the bluegrass of Kentucky—schools in Alabama and South Carolina. Dad thought we would establish our independence by moving far away for school. It worked.

None of us returned to the farm; rather, we entered our professions immediately after school: my brother—a career Army officer; my sister—a social worker/educator; and me—a career Naval officer. From a distance, my brother, sister, and I manage the farm to this day, although tobacco as a marketable crop and the cattle business have long since given way to tilling the land for wheat, corn, and soybeans.

For my part, I served thirty-two years in the Navy along with an incredibly devoted wife and two great children. Their support was foundational to my professional success. Nearly nine years of my Naval service was spent at sea on four ships. Other tours were as a staff officer at commands ashore. The Navy entrusted me with command over four units, totaling six years in charge.

The philosophy found in this work is the product of a childhood on a tobacco and cattle farm in central Kentucky, education at various schools, and a three-decade career in the U.S. Navy while simultaneously contributing as a husband, father, and grandfather. The remainder of this book will be separated into phases reflective of the major changes in my life: the farm, schooling, and a Navy career continuum from junior officer through flag officer. The lessons learned in earlier phases were often exported and applied later. The ever-increasing levels of responsibility served to teach new lessons. There are occasional farm yarns, school tales, and sea stories added to illustrate practical application of the farm philosophy, education, and Navy leadership lessons I learned along the way. I hope you enjoy the book.

JTP

CHAPTER 1

FARM FAMILY BACKGROUND

Our parents were born in the 1920s, and their worldview was formed by the Great Depression and World War II. All four of our grandparents were born in the 1800s. We have an antique way of viewing the world, I think. Dad and his family were hill people, and he had six siblings. He secured his father's permission and left his eastern Kentucky home of Tallega at age fifteen to make his way in the world. He lived above his sister and brother-in-law's grocery store in Lexington, Kentucky delivering groceries to earn his keep as he traversed high school in a strange city. Mother was from a middle-class family of long-standing Lexingtonians—the daughter of a tire company owner and one of nine children with eight surviving to adulthood.

Mother's home was less than a block away from Dad's grocery and domicile. Dad was a couple of years older than my mother, so Mom and Dad didn't socialize in high school. After high school, Dad spent four years in the Army as a paratrooper in the 11th Airborne Division—one year was spent in the war in the Pacific theater and three years in occupied Japan. Mother volunteered in various community activities to support the fight against Nazi Germany and Imperial Japan. Dad returned from the war, tried his hand at work in the North to include semi-professional baseball and basketball, returned to Lexington, and took a job at a local tire mercantile—Taylor Tire Company owned by my mother's father—our grandfather. Mother often did administrative work at the tire company, which is where she met and got to know Dad.

My parents married in the mid-1950s. My older brother was born the next year. Our sister was born four years into their marriage and I made my entrance after ten years of marital bliss. Over time, Dad worked his way into the vice president's position at the tire company. We lived in a small stone house on some land my grandfather had near a spot called Avon, Kentucky. At my grandfather's death, our family was bequeathed 200 acres of uncleared land on the other side of the farm, and shortly after—my father left the tire business to commit to full-time farming.

Mom and Dad came from opposite poles in respect to their religious upbringings. Dad was raised in an Evangelical church as a child in the hills where there was a puritanical intensity inside his mother's home. My grandmother allowed no alcohol in the house. In addition, any accoutrements that could be converted to games of chance were also prohibited. That meant no dice and no cards. Needless to say, there were no all-night Monopoly games when we went to visit Grandma in the hills. Ironically, the men would pass a bottle or jar semi-openly outside my grandmother's home—near a street light by the gravel road in front of her place. It seemed to me Grandma Palmer simply pretended not to see the outdoor activity she prohibited within her Christian home.

Our mother was from a long-standing Episcopalian family in Lexington where alcohol (especially bourbon), tobacco, and the like were all social norms. In my youth, Episcopalians were often called "Whiskey-palians" given their proclivity to provide the full spectrum of hospitality at their social events. Still, Mother should not be seen as taking her faith lightly. Mom was a true believer to the core, and Dad was an easy convert to Mom's church. I think he liked the quiet, contemplative nature of the liturgy, and he loved Anglican music. As such, ours was a religious family that attended events at church several times each week. My folks sang in the choir, volunteered to visit the sick on Sunday afternoons, and served on the church vestry (governing board). As children, we served as choristers, acolytes, and youth group participants.

Dad (second from right) and his siblings in Tallega, Kentucky, in the 1930s. Four boys (including my father) served in WWII. Only three returned.

Mom (center) with three of her older siblings in Lexington in the 1930s

School was very important. Mother was an elementary school teacher and monitored our schoolwork. Dad never went to college but addressed the importance of education at every meal reminding all of us we were to study hard so we might receive a college education. "Farmisms"—often the language foundation for farm philosophy were part of our work environment in the fields, but once under Mother's roof, we spoke English—proper English.

Farm work was important as well with a tobacco crop, cattle, chickens, and sometimes hogs requiring our attention. However, Dad did not mind temporary periods away from farm work if the competing business was educational or religious. Sports had their place, but it was a distant priority behind the church, the farm, and the schoolhouse. It was somewhat difficult to play sports as a farm kid as most of the practices and games took place in town—thirty minutes away. Our parents supported us, but it was clearly a secondary priority. I believe sports were an easy activity for our father. Although he was raised in an isolated area in eastern Kentucky, the fact he was ambidextrous permitted him to learn various sports and excel quickly—sufficient for him to be a paid basketball and baseball player after the war. My sense from him was if sports did not come easily, we were to put them aside for primary considerations: farm, church, school.

Farm fortunes were mercurial. We weren't poor, but neither were we "well-off." On good crop years, with good weather, we had cash flow but little savings. When weather was poor, tobacco was not selling for a good price, or beef prices were down, we struggled. Mother was a teacher ranging from full time work to a part-time substitute as she aged. She also served as the family bookkeeper. Dad had other business interests—landscaping and some real estate endeavors. He and mother were quite active in the community beyond the church. Dad was an elected city councilman, a Master Mason, a leader (potentate) with the local Shriners, and he was well known in the county.

Where mother was bookish and more introverted, Dad was extremely adept socially. He "never met a stranger" and was completely at ease meeting new people, speaking in public, sharing in debate, and taking a stand. As such, he insisted upon his children having the confidence to engage others, to speak publicly, to advance opinions, and debate merits. Debate of ideas was a constant in our home—especially around the dinner table.

While Dad respected a well-articulated argument, he held no such admiration for public protest where a person's only debate tactics were confined to screaming and waving signs. To be sure, he believed in the First Amendment, but he did not countenance a loud rabble. People who could not articulate their beliefs calmly and coolly in a public forum were either uninformed or weak-minded in the eyes of my father. In the same light, Dad admonished us to keep our emotions in check. He advised that to show emotion or to lose control of your emotions was a weakness, and emotionally unstable people were easily manipulated. As a result, my siblings and I developed the skill of maintaining self-control and "out-cooling" others who were predisposed to surrendering their argument's merits to the fleeting satisfaction found in an impassioned outburst.

In front of my grandfather's stone house (and my first home) on the original farm in the late 1960s. Pictured with Mom, Dad, my elder siblings

The Kentucky Palmers were a patriotic family. Both sides had a history of military service in past wars. My father's family was a gold-star family as his brother was killed in Normandy in World War II. Dad and two other brothers served and survived. Mother's brother was a soldier in the European theater who was rescued from a Nazi POW camp nearly at the point of death. He became a priest after the war. As you might imagine, the level of national sacrifice in our family was palpable, so you were unlikely to hear anything but high praise for the USA and her guardians in our house. Although, my siblings and I were born in the 50s and 60s, very little counter-culture influence made it to our farm in Avon, Kentucky.

My brother was the eldest child, and he was the "golden boy" of the farm. He loved it, took to it enthusiastically, and my parents delighted in his ability to embrace the hard work ever before us. My sister was three years junior to our brother. She was slightly more indifferent to the work but always willing to do her part. I was nine and six years junior to my brother and sister respectively. I was more of a Tom Sawyer type of farm kid. I could do the work, would do the work, but I was also looking for fun diversions in lieu of the work. While that didn't sit too well with Mom and Dad sometimes, we found our balance, and we all pulled together at the appropriate times to press forward the farm and family business interests. For me, my first eighteen and formative years were on that farm, and the lessons were plenty.

CHAPTER 2

LESSONS FROM THE FARM

LIFE ISN'T FAIR

Dad would often tear asunder any idea that life is or should be a fair endeavor. He would go on to say everyone begins life from a different starting point, and there is nothing that can be done about it. A son or daughter of the Kennedys of Massachusetts had economic advantages my father did not have as a child of Depression-era Appalachia. Nevertheless, Dad would say you should always strive and compete because in America—the most prosperous nation in the world—you can achieve anything if you're willing to put in the work. Conversely, Dad would say if you cannot succeed in America, you were unlikely to make it anywhere, so no excuses, no self-pity, no blaming others.

LIFE IS HARD—BY DESIGN

I was raised in a Christian home, and Mother was a believer—an old-school Episcopalian, a voracious reader, and a student of the Scripture and apologists. When troubles and challenges presented themselves, she would remind us how we squandered our chance at paradise on earth with the fall of man through original sin. Genesis taught us mankind was cast out of paradise, the ground was cursed, and only through toil and the sweat of our brow would humans derive sustenance—having to battle thorns and thistles among the various other punishments levied upon Adam and Eve.[1]

Mother's message: There is no utopia in the present nor will there be in our earthly future. Encountering problems, sometimes tragedy, is the lot of humans on earth, and we will continue to encounter them throughout our lives. Keep the faith, make good choices, and keep working and striving to navigate the hurdles in life. They've been placed there by the Almighty on purpose, but there is nothing asked of you that you cannot do through persistence and faith. Embrace the challenges in life. There is honor in facing your problems, adapting to them, and overcoming them. There is an equal measure of dishonor in quitting in the face of challenges and obstacles.

YOU ARE THE PRODUCT OF YOUR CHOICES

Mom and Dad were big on hard work and achievement. Their message: "What you become in life is on you and completely within your control." Although life isn't fair, America has a public school system, and with application of diligent effort, all citizens are afforded an opportunity to learn the basics in reading, writing, and arithmetic. With the basics, continued hard work, and the right choices; my father believed (and taught us) you could work your way to success. He believed it because he lived it as a son of Appalachia who left the hills as a teenager to make his way in the world during the Depression.

The book *The Millionaire Next Door* chronicles the path to wealth for the average, hardworking, and ultimately well-off American citizen. The book shows us how with good choices, self-discipline, and living within one's means, a person of modest annual earnings can amass a small fortune of greater than a million dollars in net worth. The book also shows the higher propensity for first- and second-generation immigrants to achieve significant wealth. They immigrate from nations with little and are hyper-motivated to leverage the opportunity the U.S. affords. In short, they often outwork and apply more rigid self-discipline to their activities.[2] In

America's free-market economy with the associated economic mobility, one's end state is largely a product of hard work and the series of choices one makes during the productive years of life.

Dad surveying the farm in Avon, Kentucky, in the 1970s
(Photo by Thomas H. Palmer)

SOCIETY DEMANDS A TOLL

This one comes from my brother, and it really highlights the capstone of "life isn't fair" and "you are the product of your choices." All men and women pay a toll to transit through life in America. The toll is hard work. You can pay your toll early, when you have energy and youth on your side, or you can pay it later. One pays an early toll—during their productive years of life by making good choices: finishing school, getting a job before marriage, marriage before children, living a life within their means, saving for a rainy day, saving for a home, and so on.

The model is uncomplicated and time-tested. However, if you squander your youth, drop out of school, have children before establishing the mechanisms to care for children, or simply lack the self-discipline to manage your time and resources, you will wind up paying the toll much later in life when age, energy, and time are not on your side. One might find oneself old, poor, and doing hard work for low pay or worse—subsisting off of the work of others. The bottom line is the "product of your choices" includes how early a man or woman begins to take life's choices seriously.

Bottle-feeding a calf on our back steps with my faithful first dog, Socks.

WORK IS WORK

My grandmother from the eastern Kentucky hills taught this lesson to her children and to her grandchildren. Work is work. Work is not play. Work is often not fun—not meant to be fun. Work can be arduous drudgery, but it is an absolute necessity. My nineteenth-century grandmother and Depression-era parents had absolutely no patience for a person who could work but would not. But also, work was honest, it was clean, it revealed the measure of a man or woman, required and reinforced one's character, and it unmasked the charlatan and the scoundrel.

"TO BE BEHOLDEN TO NO ONE"

This lesson comes from the hill people in Kentucky. You are responsible for you and yours. The worth of a human in society was first determined by their willingness and ability to do their part—"their job" and support themselves. You and you alone were responsible for the welfare of yourself, your family, your children, and indigent blood relatives. Debt was dangerous because in agrarian dominated America, it could cost a farmer his land. Furthermore, the specter of the "company store" in coal communities was pervasive in their ability to issue credit to coal miners beyond their means of repayment—effectively binding mining families to the coal company.

The church could help a down-and-out parishioner because neighbors supported the church, and neighbors should help neighbors in the biblical spirit. In my father's mountain world view, this did not extend to the government on any level. For a person to rely upon the government—to be "on the dole" was to be living off the sweat of someone else's brow—someone you did not know. Being under government support was shameful in the eyes of late nineteenth-century/early twentieth-century rural America. To my father, it was analogous to stealing. To borrow a line from the hill people—a prayerful appeal to heaven was for the family "to be beholden to no one."

WORK IS A BLESSING

Work or employment permits one to care for themselves and their families—the first priority for an adult. There is no shame to manual labor, farm work, trade work, or factory work. All work is valuable from the street sweeper to the town mayor. One should never be shamed or ashamed of a job well done. Whether designing the ditch or digging the ditch—both efforts were worthy of a healthy dose of pride and admiration.

PRIDE IS A SIN

Humility grounds humans. It permits them to keep perspective. It opens their hearts to faith, the condition of their fellow man, and to an understanding that personal wants, desires, and achievements are secondary to family, faith, and country. Pride is "the great sin" according to Christian apologist C. S. Lewis.[3] A small measure of pride is necessary for success, but it must be controlled. Otherwise, an overabundance of sinful pride is corrosive to character and all-consuming to the soul.

A GOOD MAN WORKS UNTIL THE DAY IS DONE

My brother says our grandmother told him "The ability to work all day is a skill." The ability to do manual labor for an entire day was a learned skill. Pace and persistence see you through to the end of the task and the end of the day. Early exhaustion was a common end-state for slackers or people unfamiliar with daily outdoor work—city folks trying their hand at farm work for the first time. Fun to watch—messy to clean up. A youngster exposed to all-day requirements of manual labor will find future office work easier and preferable by comparison. The foundation of hard work in one's early years will grow into appreciation for professional work as an adult.

"'SORRY' DON'T GET THE HAY IN THE BARN"

This is farm talk for "no excuses" for a job left undone. From a literal point of view, the hay process (for baled hay) requires hay (tall grass) to be cut, raked, baled, loaded, transported to the barn, unloaded, and stacked in the barn without getting wet. Wet or damp hay harbors mold, and it is hazardous to some livestock. Therefore, farmers "make hay while the sun shines." Farm families know the hay is essential to feeding livestock through the winter and losing hay to rain or moisture is simply not an option. If you failed to complete the process to "get the hay in the barn" it would likely get moisture on it, and the hay would be ruined. You would have to purchase hay from other farmers to sustain your livestock in the winter. As such, "'Sorry' don't get the hay in the barn."

NO ONE WORKS HARDER THAN THE FARMER'S KIDS

This was my first exposure to what would be a fundamental military leadership precept: "Leadership by example." When you're the son or daughter of a land-owning farmer, you wind up working shoulder to shoulder with hired workers to plant, harvest, house or strip tobacco, work cattle, maintain farm infrastructure, etc. The hired workers could range from fellow farm kids, to city-born college students looking to make some quick money, to adults who need the money for their families. There was also the occasional worker addicted to alcohol or drugs looking for enough income to fuel a party in the evening after work. Often times, fellow workers were strangers we didn't know "from Adam's housecat," and some of the new faces might last only for a day or a portion of a day.

Hired workers do not typically seek to work harder than the blood relatives of the land owner. As such, the pace for the work is set by the farmer's kids. Farm kids are in charge when the owner is not present. When Dad was off the farm, the chain of command defaulted to us. This drove the need for developing asymmetric leadership because fellow teenagers and grown adults (hired to do manual labor) do not respond to the yelling of the farmer's kids—whom they see as privileged—exercising the power of positional authority.

So, what to do? *Lead by example and set the pace*, because remember: "No one works harder than the farmer's kids." But, some of the hired workers will often stay close. There is an implicit challenge among workers doing physical labor to try to keep up with the other hands in pace and production. This is why it is important for the farmer's kids to set a brisk work pace, but not exhaust themselves or other workers because "the ability to work all day is a skill." You can also keep fellow coworkers off balance with conversation and humor. Yarns and tall tales go a long way toward passing the time doing tough work. As you will see in later chapters, these asymmetric leadership skills proved especially valuable as a young Naval officer leading divisions on my first ships. Why? Because just like farm kids temporarily in charge of farm operations, leadership tactics employing non-judicious screaming by a privileged (college-boy) Naval officer yields ineffective leadership, low morale, and poor performance.

"GET YOUR BOOKS"

Education permits you to work off the farm. "Get your books" was my father's daily admonition as we left for school and when we returned home. You can go anywhere, be anything you want to be with the benefit of education. Farm work was honest and honorable, but there were easier paths to supporting oneself, and supporting yourself was a primary directive for rural folk. Those easier paths were revealed through education.

EDUCATE YOUR WAY OFF THE FARM, BUT BE PREPARED TO GO BACK

Mom and Dad believed in hard work, education, and the church—end of story. Dad always told us to be "good with your hands." No matter how far you excelled or how much you achieved, you had to have the ability to work the fields, grow your own food, build things, repair equipment, and support yourself. In times of national emergency, war, family tragedy, or economic depression, my father would say you must be prepared and have the ability to return to the land—to the farm, and support yourselves and your family. I never anticipated an actual situation that would give us cause to return to the farm. However, the COVID-19 pandemic was ongoing at the time of this writing, and I must say—my father's words were echoing in my ears. I began to think through how and when we might have to "go back."

Our two main sources of income: cattle in the foreground and one of our two tobacco barns in the distance

CITY RULES DON'T APPLY TO FARM KIDS

Farm kids are unleashed on the fields at an early age and are an independent lot as a result. I learned to drive in grade school and could be observed frequently on country roads driving cars, trucks, and farm equipment—barely seeing over the steering wheel. I was given my first gun at around eight years of age—as I recall, a Harrington & Richardson single-shot 410 shotgun. I was left alone on the farm often to do work if other members of the family were away at work or school. We cared for tobacco and corn crops, a sizable family garden, cattle, pigs, and chickens. We were instructed how to use firearms safely. We were also warned about the potential need to defend ourselves with the guns we kept in the house if a stranger with unknown or bad intentions approached. I often hunted small game after school—on my own. In winter months, our firearms were also necessary to ward off roaming packs of feral dogs from attacking our newborn calves.

When farm kids turn into teenagers, they act older than their age in many ways—good and bad. The typical farm kid works hard and plays hard. Most can drive an array of vehicles, ride dirt bikes, hunt, fish, shoot well, work with livestock, ride horses, and they're typically a lean and fit lot. As stated earlier, we worked with family but also with hired strangers. Some would show up in the morning clearly under the influence from the night before—or as we would whisper, "drunker than Aunt Prissy's cow." In the course of their work, farm kids and the hired laborers might gather to work the fields, drive tractors, handle heavy equipment, tend to livestock, or climb to the top of tobacco barns where the summer sun against the tin roof sends the temperatures far beyond 100 degrees Fahrenheit. As the sun dipped below the horizon on the workday, the adults and farm kids (performing as adults) shared the spoils of hard work—often a beer and perhaps a smoke as a measure of bonding before going home and starting the workday anew at dawn. As such, many farm kids experience chewing tobacco, cigarettes, and their first sip of alcohol while in grade school.

As one might imagine, the rules for city kids including sidewalks, crossing guards, riding your bike until you're sixteen, organized sports, public transportation, fenced playgrounds, and reaching the age of twenty-one before you drink alcohol are all somewhat foreign to farm kids. They're not easily constrained and restrained by city norms, so you sometimes find the farm kid as the perceived wild child in a crowd. Most of the time, they're simply ahead of their time.

THE WELL-WORN PATH IS WELL WORN FOR A REASON

And the reason is—it works. It is proven. It is safe. It is reliable. This is a lesson I took literally as a young farmer and figuratively into my professional life after college as it related to processes, and this we will discuss later. Literally and from a farm perspective, farmers spend much of their lives traveling over uneven ground, on shaky footing, and crossing streams that can cause a truck or tractor to be stuck. A twisted ankle for a walking farmer holds the same penalty as a stuck tractor for a riding farmer. The penalty—you must spend valuable time restoring yourself and your equipment to normal operations, and this is time that could be spent on much-needed work. As such, you stick to the well-worn path, roadway, stream crossing, path across fields free of holes and stumps and so on. There is a time and a place to cross unknown ground, but you need to be sure because precious time, health, and sometimes valuable equipment can be hanging in the balance.

One of Dad's grandchildren gaining valuable tractor time under the watchful eye of Pappy

IT'S LIKE OPENING A CAR DOOR FROM THE HINGE-SIDE—YOU CAN DO IT, BUT YOU TEAR A LOT OF STUFF UP

This is the penalty for straying from the well-worn path, failing to plan, and meeting time-critical milestones. Farmers may seem as though they're players in a simple life, but farm operations are quite complex, and farmers are very self-aware. A silly or transient diversion from proven procedures on the farm (the well-worn path) can create havoc. Failure in maintaining your equipment as required, properly caring for your livestock, procuring seed, applying timely fertilizer or herbicide, even forgetting to close a gate can result in disaster. The good farmers are good planners. They understand the seasons, the fields, the crops, the required rotation, chemicals that fertilize and mitigate pests, and when labor will and will not be required. Everything is tempered by something completely out of their control—the weather. As such, farmers like to control everything they can to leverage the seasons and the weather when it is favorable. If you're a week late in planting or harvesting, it can cost the farmer dearly. Still, with all the hard work, planning, and following the well-worn path—there may still be lean times.

"WASTE NOT, WANT NOT" AND "SAVE FOR A RAINY DAY"

These puritanical admonitions are pervasive in rural America and especially on the farm. Why? There will be lean times. Conserving resources is difficult for anyone, but saving for a rainy day is especially difficult for farmers. Again—why? Do they lack self-discipline? No, most farmers are appropriately conservative, but the task is a challenging one. The business environment dictates that farmers often have to go into some level of debt to procure the material required to carry off operations over the next season or year (seed, young livestock, equipment, fertilizer, etc.). This is compounded by the fact that cashflow for farmers is inconsistent and a function of some variables which are out of their control (e.g., weather, blight, disease, market prices).

All farmers have in their recent past a poor weather year or a sickness that negatively impacted their operations and return on investment. This situation is compounded if you're a farmer whose land is leveraged by debt either to a mortgage or notes written with the land as collateral. "Putting money by" is a luxury not all farmers can enjoy, but it is a key risk-mitigation, sometimes making the difference between keeping your land or losing it.

Attending my nephew's graduation with my brother (left) and sister (center)—Farm Partners

CHAPTER 3

TALL TALES FROM THE BACK PORCH

EXTENDED FAMILY—RELATIONSHIPS MATTER

Mom and Dad had three children—my brother, my sister, and me. But more so, they raised a couple dozen other kids and young adults. These were friends, coworkers, church associates, Boy Scouts, fellow farmer friends, city neighbors, and cousins. To enable the farm operations and business endeavors involved in outdoor work, Mom and Dad hired an array of helpers from children of lifelong friends to (as I've mentioned) complete strangers. Some were looking for money, and some were sent there by their parents to engage in good clean work under Mom's and Dad's tutelage. A few lost jobs as young adults and needed the work for family support. None worked permanently for a career, but they all worked—some for a few days; some off and on for years. Some we didn't see much outside their working hours, but for a dozen or so, they were grafted into our family for life.

They might spend summers living on the farm. We could never be certain who would be at the breakfast table in the morning—our cousins from Tennessee, relatives from the hills, my brother's fraternity brothers, my sister's church camp buddies, a new acquaintance, or some combination thereof. We were bonded by hard work, clean air, cattle, tobacco, good humor, the challenges of figuring out the problems of the day, and each day ended on the back porch with some good food complete with iced tea, wine, or beer.

It was on the back porch where this extended family learned about generosity and faithfulness of our mother and the sage farm wisdom of our father. Even when the extended family members moved on to education and other careers (and to noteworthy success), they came back on weekends and holidays to reconnect with some honest work, perhaps hunt the farm, or maybe just to reconvene on the back porch. These extended family members made up the wedding parties for my siblings and me (our Tennessee cousin was my best man).

We all welcomed each other's kids to this ever-growing family and to the farm. My daughter and son used to love going to "Pappy's farm" and marveled at the numbers of people who would stop by to see my parents. The grandkids benefited greatly from the farm and some back porch time with Nana and Pappy. As for our extended family of relatives and friends, they were around over the many years while my brother and I served in the Army and Navy. They helped as my parents aged and needed assistance. They spoke, sang, and served as pall bearers at their funerals. Some even helped us stand the watch with Dad as he fought the good fight in his final months. In fact, at my dad's death, my brother and I were living out of town, and my sister was exhausted from taking care of our father. She was spending some time at home with her family. A former-farm-family member was with our dad in his last moments. He was the one to give us the sad news.

My dad's wake had over a hundred people in attendance at a local pub he used to frequent in his old age. The Episcopal priest announced the upcoming event during Dad's funeral saying: "If it surprises you that a post-funeral reception will be held at a pub, you didn't know Howard Palmer well enough to attend." But it was well attended. There was a menagerie of clergy and church-goers, Free Masons and Shriners, city officials, farmers, hill people, and of course the family. The event was fueled by farm stories many of which were told by our extended family members. In balance, our parents built much more than a farm, or a business, or a family—

they built relationships that exist even to this day in the pleasant memories of so many friends. Not a bad legacy to be sure.

"COULD YOU PLEASE FIRE ME, MR. PALMER?"

The lessons mentioned above outline our dad's brand of rugged individualism. To be certain, his worldview was forged by a childhood in the hills, and the only countermeasure to life's pressures he knew was working hard to earn and support his family. It was a simple and straightforward strategy he believed was foolproof. As mentioned previously, for an individual to spurn available work was, to my dad, an irrevocable character flaw.

I recall one short-term worker—a young man in his twenties who looked to be a product of rural Kentucky. He couldn't or wouldn't hack the farm demands my parents laid on their kids and extra hired workers. He worked a day—maybe two, drew his wages from our mother (acting as bookkeeper), and then he quit. A week later he returned to the farm to ask my father for a favor. Upon appearing out in the tobacco fields, Dad, in his usual gruff manner, said: "What the hell are you doing back here—didn't you quit last week?" At this point, all work stopped so we could observe the coming exchange. The young man, said, "Mr. Palmer, I'd like you to fire me." Dad replied, "What!? How can I fire you if you quit last week?" The former worker replied, "Well, sir, if you fire me, I can draw unemployment." Dad said: "Hell, son, you had employment just last week! Why would you want to draw unemployment?" The man reiterated he could "get his check" if fired but was due no government assistance as a worker who voluntarily quit his situation.

This is when Dad's blood boiled over. It is important to point out our father was an everyday tobacco and cattle farmer, and as such, he was muscular and fit in addition to being well over six feet in height. Even as he aged into his fifties and sixties, he was more than a physical match for most workers we encountered—including those who were decades his junior. He took delight in outworking young adults. So, when this young adult asked our dad to join his conspiracy to take advantage of government's largesse, the fuse was lit. Our father—a child of Depression-era Appalachia who still rose every day at 5 a.m. to milk and feed cattle before the work day started—had had enough. Dad told the young man in high volume that the only thing worse than being a quitter was "being an able-bodied, lazy, bum." Dad accused him in front of witnesses of being a thief and absconding with the tax dollars of hard-working Americans. Add to it that the man had the temerity to ask my father to be an active party to this "untruth" to carry off the ruse. Dad told him he should be ashamed, and he shamed him publicly.

The lesson to all assembled was clear. If you're healthy and of sound mind, your worth was tied directly to your work—period. No excuses. Perhaps Dad overplayed his hand and didn't adhere to his normal practice of protecting another man's dignity, but it was clear this former employee unknowingly crossed a painful and personal redline with my father. I would like to say there was a happy ending where the worker in question turned from his slothful ways after his interaction with Dad, but who is to say—we never saw him again.

Phoning friends and family telling them about my first shotgun

EDUCATION'S PURPOSE

Mom and Dad were great advocates of the power of education to enable self-sufficiency and improve the quality of life of one's family. As previously stated, education ranked prominently in our family trilogy of faith, farm, and school. The end game was to be self-sufficient, on your own, beholden to no one. Dad really liked the idea of us receiving at least a portion of our college far away from home in Alabama and South Carolina. He believed we would develop the independence and life skills to not return home. After completing school and as adults, Mom and Dad were always glad to see us, but there was never an invitation (implied or expressed) to return home to live. Our mission was to use hard work and education to leave the farm and make our own way. We knew the farm was available to us as an emergency option (if the economy collapsed or there was a national disaster), but otherwise, we were to "get-gone and stay-gone" from the farm. It worked, and we now operate the farm from our current homes near and far. We don't reside on the land anymore—no one does, and that makes visits to our "old Kentucky home" a little hollow. Our parents' clearly articulated vision during our upbringing was achieved through education. We educated our way off the farm and out into the world—never to return. "Well done!" to Mom and Dad.

A FINAL INSPECTION

One night, I received an odd phone call from my dad. This was a couple of years after Mother passed away, so my brother, sister, and I tried to increase our frequency of communications with our father to make certain he was alright. This night Dad said, "Son, I need you to go to a funeral." This was a rare request for me as I lived a full day's drive from Dad's home in Kentucky. My sister, living nearby the old farm typically attended central Kentucky funerals to represent the family if Dad was unable to go. In this particular case, I was charged with going to a funeral for a distant relative a few hours' drive from my duty station, but not for the reasons one might expect.

Before an untimely death, this particular relative developed a reputation for questionable behavior with some of our elderly aunts and uncles in the same age group as my dad. There were whispers of defaulted loans and pressure applied to wrest money from the lonely senior citizens in their waning years. I had no reason to believe Dad fell for any malfeasance. Still, he was aware of the reports to be sure, and they troubled him.

My father's instructions were to go to the funeral and make sure our dead relative was indeed "good and dead." Dad said he wouldn't put it past this character to fake a death to duck outstanding obligations and debts. If there was a closed casket, I was to ask for a private viewing. I made the drive after work and attended the visitation. To the assembled family and friends, I doubt many knew who I was. In an application of the old Navy lesson— "you get what you inspect, not what you expect," I confirmed the untimely passing and reported the situation back to my father. He was pensive about the loss, but relieved to confirm the truth. This is one unique inspection I have never had to repeat and never will forget.

PASSING THE TORCH

One of the last times I saw my dad do work on the farm was him working with his grandson—my son. Dad had to be in his upper seventies which had to make our boy no more than twelve or maybe thirteen years old. We were visiting—staying at the old farm house, and my son came bounding into the room one morning saying "I'm going to work with Pappy today! We're moving hay." I said: "That's good—just be careful and be ready for the transformation." My son said,"What transformation?" I replied, "The transformation where your pappy will turn into my father." He looked at me quizzically, and I said, "Look, just do whatever Pappy says, and you'll be fine—have fun." My wife then grabbed me and said I was to stay within sight of Pappy and our boy as an added measure of safety. So, I pretended to be driving the farm perimeter checking fence lines (as we still had cattle on the farm) while keeping a distant eye on the farm operations of the day.

Dad had an old yellow Case tractor with a hay spear mounted to the rear hydraulics used for moving the large half-ton rolls of hay around the farm. The cattle consumed about one roll of hay per day in the winter along with crushed corn. Moving a roll or two of hay out to the cattle was a daily occurrence, but today, Dad wanted to move the remaining rolls to a field closer to the cattle for the remainder of the winter. Well, my dad pushing eighty was sitting on the back right fender of the tractor as my son, approaching his teens was driving. Dad was holding onto the roll cage with his right hand and the back of my son's driver's seat with the left. My son was doing a pretty fair job for a youngster who had only driven trucks and tractors with his pappy a few times, but when the work got complicated, Dad started giving direction. At one point, Dad was directing, his grandson wasn't getting the message as intended, he turned the tractor too sharply, and the load was going unbalanced. Dad gave him a not-so-playful whack on the back of the head to focus his attention.

Even from a distance, I could tell my son was gob-smacked to receive a physical rebuke from his normally loving and cuddly Pappy. Having been on the receiving end of my dad's "direction" many times, I must say I had a wry smile and took some perverse pleasure seeing the look on my son's face as my dad continued to give directions in his spicy farmer's vernacular while the sting from the "attention-getter" sunk in. My son did what we all did in the past—took the criticism, corrected the action, and continued the work for the remainder of the morning. At lunch, he was proud as a peacock of his work with his pappy, and Dad, never one to give faint praise, said, "The boy did okay—he can stay on for more work if he wants." Dad worked the farm as best he could for his remaining years—most of the time riding that old Case tractor.

Fast-forward about a dozen years, including seven years passing since the Lord called our dad home to be with Mom. Dad's Case tractor fell into years of disrepair. My now adult and married son pulled a flatbed trailer from his home in South Carolina to the old farm in Kentucky to claim his pappy's tractor. With some help from friends, family, and the farmer across the road, he loaded the tractor onto the flatbed. He took it to his home in South Carolina, unloaded it in his back yard, and had it started in less than twenty-four hours. He is slowly restoring the vehicle—navigating a bee's nest behind the radiator, hydraulic hoses suffering dry rot, and obsolete parts among other challenges. He has already given rides on the tractor to Pappy's great-grandchildren including our son's two daughters. The torch was figuratively passed by Pappy to his grandson when moving hay in my dad's waning years, and the tangible artifact in the form of the tractor is secure in the hands of that same grandson for the new generations to experience.

On the Avon, Kentucky, farm with my son (center) and my sister after loading Pappy's old tractor on the trailer before moving it to South Carolina

CHAPTER 4

LESSONS IN EDUCATION

EDUCATION IN KENTUCKY

My education was unusual for a farm kid. My sister was six years my senior. Throughout her elementary school years, she tried to teach her toddler brother lessons as though I was her student. Prior to elementary school, I knew the alphabet and numbers, could read simple sentences, and do rudimentary addition and subtraction. This was all reinforced by church and choir activity where you had to read music and lyrics (Latin, old English, contemporary English) to be functional. As such, I was considered smart or advanced when I reached school age. I did well early in school, and my parents, based on farm fortunes, would move me to the schools they believed would best prepare me for my future and keep me out of trouble.

By my count I attended seven schools between K–12, public and private. I attended preschool and kindergarten at our church school. The public schools were instructive. First grade and third through sixth grade were at a country elementary school catering to rural white and black children (second grade was spent at an elementary school "in town"—in Lexington). At the country elementary school (Briar Hill), some kids were poor, some not as much, and few were what I would consider well-off. This school was a model of stability as largely the same teachers taught me (in the same grades) as taught my brother and sister who were nine years and six years older. Our elementary school teachers were well known to us as they were our neighbors in a tiny area of Fayette County called Avon.

Our formative education occurred at Briar Hill Elementary School near Avon, Kentucky

Our public junior and senior high schools (both called Bryan Station) were in Lexington and were fed from the rural elementary schools and some city schools—many from the blue-collar neighborhoods. I remember long bus rides to school, lots of diversity, and the opportunity to learn and coexist with others who were from different backgrounds. My sense is Mom and Dad liked to keep me off balance with school, so they moved me around often—once in the middle of a school semester. If I slacked off or school appeared too easy, I moved. If I started running with kids they believed represented a bad influence, I moved. I intermittently attended and ultimately graduated from a private school in downtown Lexington called Sayre where I was exposed to classmates who were children of college-educated professionals. The teachers and administration were exceptional. I found the history lectures by the school's headmaster and the high school head intellectually inspiring. Physics was my favorite subject, and I added an extra year as an elective because the teacher made the subject matter an enjoyable learning experience. It was a fine education, but I did not apply myself adequately to optimize the experience—largely because "city rules" didn't apply to this farm kid. I spent more time as an adolescent pretending to be a fun-loving adult rather than a child-student making the most of my educational opportunities. A poor choice on my part. Still, I was well prepared for the next phase in my education at The Citadel, The Military College of South Carolina in Charleston.

THE CITADEL

"I wear the ring"

"I wear the ring" is the first line of a Pat Conroy work titled *The Lords of Discipline*. The book of fiction draws loosely from his experience as a student at The Citadel in the 1960s.[4] This line summarizes aptly the school, the students, and the alumni in four simple words: "I wear the ring."

The ring is a tangible symbol of gold that has remained unchanged for over a century with the exception of the annual adjustment of class-year numerals on the top. This all-but-identical band of gold pervades every element of the college and the alumni. The Citadel is a challenging environment where your worth is determined by your capacity to navigate four tough years in pursuit of "the ring." Each cadet's work is rewarded in a ring presentation in the fall of senior year followed by commencement in the spring. As one might expect, an impressive level of ceremony accompanies both events. Quite simply, to many Citadel graduates, their worldview is simple, and it is binary. You either wear the ring, or you do not, and only those who do are members of the tight fraternity. All other schools, students, and graduates are seen as wanting by comparison in the mindset of many cadets and graduates I encounter.

During my time attending The Citadel, the school had a somewhat harsh fourth-class system that by certain standards might be considered hazing today. This is especially true during the first year in the plebe system—otherwise known as "knob" year. First year, fourth-class "knobs" were so named owing to their door-knob look from the ritualistic shaving of their heads immediately upon matriculating to the school. It was a high-testosterone, rock-em/sock-em, rough-and-tumble, all-male world, and proudly so.

Women were not admitted until the mid-1990s after lengthy battles in court. Back in the all-male mid-1980s, it was a physical affair requiring fitness and resilience. Wrestling matches (sometimes devolving to fist fights) to settle personal differences were fairly common. One cadet might convey "well done" to another by thumping his counterpart's chest with a closed fist as though pounding on a thick door. I embraced the strict military regimen, benefited from the mandatory and monitored study hours each night, and did well enough to obtain a three-year Navy ROTC scholarship. I submitted to the school's rigors enthusiastically. I balanced military responsibilities as a rank holder each upper-class year, playing sports for two years (rowing and rugby), and achieving some notoriety as a senior earning a spot on an elite drill platoon called the Summerall Guards. I graduated with a Bachelor of Science degree in Business Administration that included departmental honors and designation as a Distinguished Naval Student.

Although a different world, The Citadel reinforced many of the lessons taught on our family farm—e.g., recognition that there were powers and priorities bigger than one's self, no excuse for lack of success/mission accomplishment, endurance of hardship if necessary to complete required tasks, etc. However, the school's esprit de corps among the cadets' class and assigned company (for me—Charlie Company's "Casual Cats"), attention to detail, maniacal type-A competition against one's self-imposed high standards as well as performance of one's peers, and code of honor finished nicely the process my parents started. The Citadel served as an outstanding training ground for my future Naval service. This was all in the setting of a most beautiful and hospitable city—Charleston, South Carolina. My wife and I met when I was a cadet, and she was a cross-town college student. We married a year after my graduation and honeymooned in Charleston. Our son is a Citadel alumnus as well. My cadet experience on the Ashley River was transformational, and I added many lessons to my farm kid foundation while in Charleston.

My ring and my son's ring in the fall of 2013—shortly after his presentation ceremony

Follow without fear

"Follow without fear" is a line from The Citadel's alma mater.[5] As mentioned previously, The Citadel had and still maintains a tough, adversarial fourth-class system, and one of the most foreboding challenges is "knob year." The first lesson: the school makes you face and conquer fear on day one. Your first official act is to report to your company First Sergeant. It never goes well, because knobs can do nothing right—by design. But the lesson is extremely valuable. To know there is extreme discomfort in the offing and to focus and persevere is an all too rare experience these days. Starting with the report to the First Sergeant, knobs face and navigate thousands of similar fearful hurdles and no-win situations throughout their first year. The lessons to be absorbed include—fear is normal, fear is distracting, fear can be self-defeating, but most importantly, fear is manageable. You can conquer fear.

Those who strive and compete know about fear and stress. If you look at fear as a normal and temporary state for human beings that can be navigated, then the fight-or-flight continuum tilts toward fight most of the time. Survivors face the fear and accept the challenge of the fight. If you let fear get the better of you, you are signing up for near-term defeat with long-term implications for you and your team. Fear and stress are close cousins, and stress can be constructive or destructive. I have had many opportunities where stress could have gotten me down. A few examples include twenty-hour workdays while deployed in a hostile environment at sea or leading billion-dollar organizations ashore. However, my cure for stress is "preparation." For me, nothing relieves stress quite like knowing with certainty I am well practiced and positioned to knock a tough task out of the park. The building blocks of preparation (planning, communications, etc.) are found later in this book, but the first element in the equation is facing down fear.

"Sir, Yes Sir; Sir, No Sir; Sir, No Excuse Sir"

These are the only acceptable answers first year cadets or knobs may use when answering a question from the upper classes. If asked to elaborate by an upperclassman, knobs could then expound. Though somewhat silly, the lesson learned is valuable and foundational. Keep it simple. Stick to the facts. Do not shade your answers to benefit one's position. Do not obfuscate. Get through the interaction with as much efficiency and economy of words as possible. Knob interactions with upperclassmen are more often than not heated affairs, so the simplicity of the model trains you to focus and push through any adversarial events and live to fight another day.

Home sweet home—the quadrangle, open-air galleries, and stairs of The Citadel's Murray Barracks and 1st Battalion—Charlie Company

"Suck it up like a bulldog and drive on"

The Citadel's mascot is a bulldog—simple enough, but "driving" holds many connotations. For the average citizen—"drive on" means to continue. For Citadel cadets and graduates, driving was how knobs moved on foot throughout the barracks when out of their rooms and on the open-air galleries and checkerboard quadrangle. It was an embarrassing caricature where knobs double-time, with knees high, elbows-in and forearms parallel to the galleries or "deck" with hands formed as fists—as though they were driving an invisible car. In barracks speak, you would "drive-on" to your destination, request permission to "drive-by" an upperclassman, "drive-up" or down the circular stairs leading to one of the four floors or "divisions" in one of the five, castle-image barracks—each hosting 500 cadets. As an upperclassman, when a knob rapped twice on your door requesting permission to "drive into" your room, an upper-class answer in the affirmative was, "Drive, knob!" Whenever a cadet experienced hardship or discomfort in the performance of their daily studies, sports, duties, guard duty, or physical training—the "encouragement" one received was to "Suck it up like a bulldog and drive on."

That was simple Citadel code for forget the excuses, hurdles, impediments, and whining and just continue to press forward. Remember the first line of the poem "Solitude" by Eller Wheeler Wilcox:

> Laugh and the world laughs with you;
> Weep and you weep alone.[6]

Translation: No one wants to hear your problems. The Citadel teaches you the world is indifferent to the plight of the individual not achieving the success they seek. Rather, the school trains you to redouble your efforts such that even if you fail, you have the personal consolation of knowing you gave your all in the pursuit of your goals.

"Embrace the suck"

This one is not exclusive to The Citadel, and one also hears it often in the U.S. military. "Embrace the suck" is a close cousin to "Suck it up and drive on." There is a sense of prideful accomplishment in taking on an uncomfortable challenge and outlasting it. In the case of The Citadel, "the suck" could be navigating the hundreds of no-win situations to complete knob year, facing a tough class or physical trial, or just the spartan living conditions and the time locked up on campus for classes, mandatory study, parade and ceremony, or serving punishment. In the military "the suck" is easily applicable for arduous deployments at sea or "downrange" in a hostile environment on land—away from your family, disassociated from the culture, comforts, and safety of America. It could be a simple matter of having weekend duty at your unit when your compatriots are home spending their free time with their families. In the spirit of the old phrase: "Where there is no alternative, there is no problem"—"Embrace the suck" is a modern upgrade. Complaining and worrying serve no purpose, so "Embrace the suck."

If you cannot laugh . . .

Gallows humor is the meat and potatoes of survival at The Citadel, and I think the manufactured hardship and conditioned responses are what make it a good school for those aspiring to military service. You have to find humor in uncomfortable situations. If you cannot laugh at yourself, your classmates, and the twisted situations you will face at The Citadel, you will struggle to survive. The laughter is presumed to be in the company of your classmates during knob year. Humor bonds the team, and the lesson learned is to abandon any sort of "superman" or "lone-wolf" strategy.

"Never give up, for you never know, victory may be had with just one more blow!"

Time on the farm certainly taught me the value of a job well done, persistence, working full and long days, but The Citadel took it to a new level. In August of 1984, Charlie Company's executive officer (a cadet first lieutenant) provided some motivational advice to me and the assembled class of new knobs in the barracks during "Hell Week." The statement "Never give up for you never know, victory may be had with just one more blow" has stuck with me to this day. The first year/knob year is a time of no-win situations and scenarios where missteps and punishment are a certainty. As one might expect, knobs and their classmates learn to rely upon one another in the face of three upper classes charged with administering the first-year dues that must be paid if you have any hope of earning a class ring as a senior. This is especially true in the knobs' respective companies where they live, eat, sleep, train, suffer, strive, and thrive together. The nine-month pressure cooker taught you to take the long game—and simply refuse to quit.

From a military school, fourth-class system standpoint, one could make it by simply hanging in and hanging on—most often with the help of classmates who helped carry the load when you were down, troubled, or the target of upper-class ire. These upperclassmen often espoused the unofficial motto of "Attrition is our mission!" and the mark of a good company's cadre (small group of upperclassmen in each company charged with initial training of knobs) was the culling of the herd of those who were not committed or prepared sufficiently to survive the year.

I saw many thin and wiry knobs simply bear down, focus, and live to face another day's challenges until—lo and behold—they were at the end of knob year at "Recognition Day." Recognition is the final day at the end of freshmen year for knobs when they exchange first names with the three classes senior to them and join the upper classes).

Conversely, I saw muscle-bound, hyper-fit, and pseudo-motivated knobs drop out within a week or two because they recognized it was to be nine months of suck, and they couldn't dispense with "the system" in quick fashion with a fast display of speed and strength. The Citadel in the 1980s was a laboratory for human behavior under pressure for knobs and simultaneously for upperclassmen when granted power. Some responded well, some did not—all learned lessons. The key lessons learned for those freshmen who survived the nine months as knobs were: Never quit—don't say it, don't think it—and put your trust in your classmates to help carry the load when it seems too much.

Guard your honor

The Citadel's current honor code was instituted under General Mark Clark's tenure as school president in the mid-twentieth century, and it was and is: "A cadet does not lie, cheat, or steal, nor tolerate those that do."[7] It is a simple and firm code. It was in theory a one-strike-and-you're-out program. It worked in the 1980s Citadel, although as with all things, the application of the code was sometimes imperfect. The code required a unanimous vote of guilty by a jury of cadets to achieve a conviction, and the vast majority of guilty verdicts resulted in expulsion. I was never elected to the honor committee by my classmates; however, I did successfully defend a classmate before the court.

To my recollection, the juries tended to acquit if there was doubt about the evidence, and I do not recall stories about a cadet being railroaded on shabby evidence. I remember cadets being convicted by a court of their cadet peers and expelled (or resigning under specter of conviction and expulsion) for plagiarism, petty theft, or lying about a material matter (e.g., presence during bed check or "all in"). I saw some cadets employ attorneys to help them create the best arguments possible and navigate honor court appearances successfully in cases that were rumored to be cut-and-dried.

Nevertheless, the code is integral to the cadet experience and alumni reputation. George C. Scott portraying a fictional military school superintendent in the film *Taps* provided a quote summarizing my impression of the application of honor at my alma mater: "Burglar proof, weather proof, fool proof, one hundred-proof! Honor. Everything else is subject to the powers that be. To the caprices of often inferior men. But your honor is your own, inviolate."[8] The overriding theme was you must act honorably and guard your honor at all times. It was the one thing you could neither reconstruct, resuscitate, nor rehabilitate.

Senior picture from The Citadel in 1988

CHAPTER 5

BARRACKS BANTER—TALES FROM BEHIND THE GATES AT THE CITADEL

RELY UPON YOUR CLASSMATES

As previously mentioned, navigation of the first (knob) year of the fourth-class system at The Citadel is a team game. Lone wolves are easily dispatched by the cadre—usually within a few short days or weeks. Yet, you begin the process all alone—facing your company First Sergeant at a card table in front of your company letter (painted letter on the outside stairwell wall identifying which corner of your barracks is your company's territory).

In short work, you meet your knob roommate for a scant few seconds as you put on a uniform you do not yet know how to wear, and you "toe the line" on the galleries for the first time. Each company has about thirty freshmen—all in the same predicament—nine months of "suck." Relying on your peripheral vision (you can't look around), you hear your classmates yelling out answers to questions about last name and initials—"Cadet recruit Palmer, J. T."—hometowns, why they wanted to sign up for Citadel abuse, etc.

Very quickly you start to form in your mind an impression of your thirty partners in the struggle upon which you are embarking—your company classmates. You spend the day marching around campus, standing at attention in lines, picking up books, uniforms, administrative material, learning how to set up your barracks room, initial rudiments of marching and drill, and the like. In conjunction with the first day's events, you get a few minutes here and there to whisper "hey" and form the first interactions that would become friendships with your classmates.

You learn quickly not to "sh*t_ _on" your classmates by taking the easy route at their expense, informing on their activities, hiding while there is company work to be done or punishment to be served. You also learn to form the knob team—a phalanx of college freshmen who figuratively lock arms and charge through all challenges. When one is down, the team picks him/her up. When one is having a good day, the team provides perspective. When one is in trouble, others might make mistakes intentionally and draw upper-class attention to take the heat off their classmate. There are some standout performances to be remembered. Two for me involved the tallest knob in our company.

The upperclassmen immediately gave him the counterintuitive nickname "Big Geek" which was funny because this young man was a big strapping kid from the western part of the state. We were assigned our squads by height, so as the second tallest knob in Charlie Company, I spent most of the year directly behind or beside Big Geek in formations and when marching. He was older than a typical knob making it into the Corps just under the age restriction at the time. Big Geek was a legacy knob with a big brother who graduated two years before we arrived, and he followed in his sibling's wake to The Citadel. He worked as a long-haul trucker out of high school. He was worldly, big, strong, and tough. The upperclassmen put him through his paces but always in numbers because no one wanted to take on Big Geek one-on-one. Our classmates in a neighboring company got a lesson in messing with the big man one day.

We had a pep rally on the quadrangle where the knobs from all four companies of First Battalion had to do crazy antics to get fired up for the football game. There was always competition between companies (grades, intramurals, military performance) and the different companies' knobs pulled pranks on other freshmen from time to time. Big Geek got separated from us, and the knobs in another company tried to "capture" him by pushing him into a room.

Apparently, one of the knobs said, "Let's paint our company letter on his ass with Heel & Sole (liquid shoeshine edge dressing)." That was enough for Big Geek, and at that point, he decided to fight his way out of the room—one knob against two dozen.

By the time the other Charlie Company knobs and I determined he was in trouble and attempted rescue, the situation was well in hand. We peered through the doorway and witnessed Big Geek dispatching the opposing company freshmen like a teenaged boy pushes around his toddler siblings. Big Geek grabbed, threw, tossed, punched, and cut a path out of the room in Paul Bunyan fashion. As he exited the room, a senior who was standing Officer of the Guard (OG—a senior cadet officer for the rotating watch detail for the barracks), grabbed Big Geek from behind. Big Geek, thinking the OG was another belligerent freshman, knocked the OG for a loop. Sword and cover went flying across the quad.

It was at this time two Charlie Company seniors shepherded Big Geek to one of the 250 rooms in Murray Barracks to keep him from committing further violence and to give them time to cool the anger of the recently revived OG (their fellow classmate) on the quadrangle. From that point on, Big Geek was a knob the upper classes handled carefully. To be sure, he did his time in sweat parties, PT runs, pre-formation push-ups, etc. But the upper classes had their eye on a time in May when Big Geek would be able to call out upperclassmen for a "bury the hatchet" wrestling match at the end of freshman year during the annual company party at the beach.

Big Geek ran cover for us from time to time. I got cross-wired with a sophomore corporal whom I called a pejorative name (on the orders of a junior sergeant), and I was put on moto-mess for two weeks. Motivational "moto-mess" was a table reserved for knobs who needed a lesson or to be motivated because of misdeeds—you get scant food on moto-mess. Over the two weeks, Big Geek (at some risk) smuggled food for me from the mess hall into the barracks past the inspections of the OG and his team standing guard.

Big Geek leaned on us too. He required a little help negotiating some of the academic subjects, and we took turns helping him through some of the tougher classes over his four years on the Ashley River. Big Geek graduated on time, and we keep in touch. There is no doubt if ever I need assistance, money, or help getting out of a tight spot—today as it was back then—Big Geek would be on the road in about ten minutes to help fix the problem. Moreover, many of us would do the same for him as well as our other Charlie Company "Casual Cat" classmates. It's part of the code and a fundamental lesson in teamwork—"rely upon your classmates"—they'll see you through any problem.

PERFECTING THE LAUGHTER—"RUNNING SH*T_ _"

As stated previously, a sense of humor was an absolute necessity for a first-year, fourth class cadet. The gallows humor pervasive throughout the Corps and especially within the knob class was used to combat meager feeding (I got down to 142 pounds as a knob standing six feet three inches), dozens of no-win situations followed by push-ups, double-timing, and "stereo" (upperclassmen screaming simultaneously in either ears giving countermanding orders drawing more push-ups, etc.). This was all accompanied by a stringent academic environment where professors were largely unaware or indifferent to the challenges in the barracks. If not for the sacrosanct hours of evening study period, all would have flunked out.

After hell week (the first week) was a two-month period where knobs carry the title "Cadet-Recruits." This phase ended on Parents' Day (usually in early October) when knobs transitioned from Cadet-Recruits (subject only to the orders of a handful of rankholders in their companies called the cadre) to "Cadet-Privates." The newly anointed Cadet-Privates were subject to the eyes and orders of all 1,500 cadets of the upper three classes. Knobs were understandably thrilled to see their parents on Parents' Day, but they knew from barracks lore they were going to face a whirlwind of aggressive upperclassmen who waited only semi-patiently for their first sanctioned opportunity to extract their pound of flesh from the newly installed privates.

By October, the cohesive collections of knobs in each company formed the bonds that made a resilient unit against the upper three classes and they survived—then they thrived—then they began to engage in another tradition of knobs practicing anonymous pranks on upperclassmen or in Citadel parlance— "running sh*t." Examples could include after-Taps hit-and-run shaving cream bombs. There were the prank phone calls to the cadets on guard duty with a spot-on imitation of the army officer commandant directing a mid-night inspection of an upperclassman's room for contraband. There were disappearances of furniture and mattresses, thin layers of oil on smooth pavement causing upperclassmen to slip and fall on the galleries, and fifty-gallon rubber trashcans filled with water and leaned against a room door so that when the door is opened inward, the room was flooded with water. There were even stories of upperclassmen having their rooms bricked in by knobs performing as amateur masons quietly throughout the night.

For those of us in 1st Battalion, Charlie Company, one example was a satirical "Geek of the Week" exposé posted on the company bulletin board every week or so in the wee hours of the morning. In a pre-personal computer environment, the handwritten list had to be printed in block letters to preclude the identification of the author(s). It was a short list of upperclassmen, editorializing unfortunate recent circumstances (rule breaking), a physical attribute (freckles, tall/thin, short/stumpy, nerd/jock, etc.), or a relationship event (hookup/breakup/engagement). Upperclassmen would crowd around the bulletin board, read the article, howl in laughter, make fun of the upper-class geeks of the week (GOW), and then we freshmen would get dropped for a ton of push-ups we were going to have to do anyway for any number of "infractions."

One particular edition had a lasting effect on me. I helped to pen the GOW one night, and we emulated the "Beauty of the Week" passage from the school's newspaper that normally profiled a cadet's girlfriend with a photo and short bio to include school, hobbies, turn-ons, and turn-offs. The GOW victim was a Charlie Company senior who had been taking some ribbing from his classmates for dating a hometown girl who was just eighteen. We identified the cadet as well as his girlfriend's name and used as the beauty of the week photo the famous "Coppertone" suntan lotion image. The iconic image consisted of a puppy pulling down the shorts of a female toddler exposing a small portion of her backside with a tan line revealed. As I recall, we listed her hobbies as hopscotch, pretend tea parties, and playing with dolls. Turn-ons were recess and nap-time. Turn-offs referenced her boyfriend's cologne being the same as her daddy's, and her education was described as "early elementary."

Geek of the Week photo of the satirical "Beauty of the Week"

The edition was well received by the upperclassmen who were not listed; however, the cadet GOW who had his girlfriend pseudo-profiled as beauty of the week was furious. Through some sleuthing and amateur handwriting analysis, he figured out I was one of the authors of the most recent GOW list. He swore vengeance but saved all his anger for the last parade of the year which was traditionally followed by Recognition Day.

Recognition Day consists of a gut-busting physical training (PT) period where freshmen, in their last act as knobs, are worked to exhaustion. PT is followed by "recognition" by the upperclassmen complete with handshakes and exchanging first names for the first time after nine months of giving and taking everything you have for your company, your class pride, and your knob classmates. Recognition is the end of knob year, and there is no better feeling, but like most things at The Citadel, you have to pay a price for your privilege.

Looking back, we all got a good laugh from the GOW editions, but I paid a healthy bounty of physical training that afternoon on the quad under the direction of the aforementioned geek of the week. I can assure you I richly earned my recognition handshakes and congratulations.

OPERATIONAL SECURITY—THEY NEVER KNEW MY BIRTHDAY

My first lessons in Operational Security (OPSEC) were in college. The Citadel is a funny place full of an array of traditions. One such tradition was helping a fellow cadet celebrate his birthday. Normal college birthday celebrations might conjure images of pizza and beer with a few friends, an intimate dinner with a significant other, or perhaps a fraternity keg party on a brother's twenty-first birthday. Not at The Citadel. Our traditions were analogous to a mother lion pawing her cubs to teach them a lesson in humility when a member of a pride steps out of line—or in this case when an upper-class cadet in the Corps ages another year.

School-year birthdays were guarded as though national secrets. Why? The "tradition" that existed for the upper three classes (sophomore, junior, and senior) was your own classmates would wait for "tattoo" (a bugle call signaling the end of evening study period at 10:30 p.m.), take the birthday boy out to the middle of the barracks quadrangle, strip him, tie him to a chair, and then return to the galleries (the four stories of surrounding square balconies) and serenade them with "Happy Birthday."

At the sounds of "Happy Birthday," all three upper classes from all four companies in that particular barracks would explode onto the galleries and join in the serenade followed by about fifteen minutes of pelting the birthday cadet with shaving cream bombs, tobacco spit, city phonebooks (that no one used), and flaming paper airplanes. Various other artillery might include fruits and vegetables smuggled into the barracks after the evening meal, trash, half-full soda cans, and maybe a urine bomb or two if the birthday boy engendered an enemy recently.

Your "party" ended only when you could wriggle out of your bonds. If you were unable to free yourself, a benevolent classmate would send a squad of knobs out to the center of the quad on a "rescue mission." The knobs had to dodge the same artillery fire and conduct you to the safety of the galleries, where you could free yourself from the chair and dash to the nearest shower to wash off all your "celebration." The tradition was semi-good-natured fun—but not much fun for the birthday boy.

On a practical note, I learned pain, discomfort, and embarrassment are motivators, but they are hardly constructive. The birthday tradition motivated many to keep secret an otherwise positive life event. After witnessing a half-dozen birthday celebrations as a knob (knob birthdays were not celebrated in this fashion), I was determined my January birthday would remain a secret until graduation—and it did.

Charlie Company Class of '88 Seniors after ring ceremony

HONOR—LETTING YOUR GUARD DOWN

I had an honor code scare in my second year. I held a position (company clerk) requiring many visitors to our room from all classes. My fellow clerk roommate and I had an array of abandoned material, and our clerk's office acted as a pseudo lost-and-found. It included uniform items, athletic equipment, an occasional pair of glasses, and a parcel of books left in our room for several weeks as we approached the end of my sophomore year. We included the books in the twice-daily announcements to the rest of Charlie Company about items lost and found in our office. No one claimed the books.

In the chaos of the end of the school year, cadets trade, sell, or throw away books, uniforms, and personal items as they prepare to lighten their load for graduation or a return home for summer furlough followed by the next year at school. As such, industrial dumpsters were placed in each barracks quadrangle, and they soon overflowed. The unclaimed books could have been simply tossed in one of the dumpsters as we cleaned out our room. However, there was an end-of-year common practice where cadets could take the books to the student bookstore to ascertain if they could be sold back to the store for sale to cadets the following school year.

I had a handful of my personal books in addition to the unclaimed books we considered abandoned, and I was headed to the bookstore to see if any were on the list for sell-back. On the way out of the barracks I was stopped by another cadet (the owner of the unclaimed books). He inquired: "Where are you going with those books?" I replied, "I'm taking books to the bookstore to see if any are eligible for sell-back." I realized immediately I was not giving a complete and accurate depiction. I immediately reversed myself and clarified that some of the books were not purchased by me, but they were unclaimed books left in our room for some weeks.

The other cadet identified them has his books and took them back to his room. It turns out his roommate borrowed the books and inadvertently left them in our room when passing through several weeks earlier. What I thought were abandoned books were actually perceived to be lost or stolen books by the rightful owner.

Had I not had a chance encounter with the owner on the way to the bookstore buy-back session, I may have sold one or more of the books and then undergone examination under the strict honor code. The fact of the matter was the books were his and not abandoned textbooks. Had I converted some of them to cash, I would have had difficulty explaining how my actions were anything but thievery. It was a close call.

The owner of the books was satisfied I did not steal his property when his roommate confirmed he inadvertently left them in our room those many weeks before. The brush with a potential honor investigation and possible court proceeding—carrying the penalty of expulsion, loss of a Navy scholarship and future career as a Naval officer reinforced in me the absolute necessity to always have my "antenna attuned" to guard against any possible breaches of honor—intentional or otherwise. I would, for the rest of my cadet and professional careers advise my charges to "Guard your honor—at all times—at all cost."

Wearing a shako with plume and marching at the head of the 1988 Summerall Guards as Front Guide

ENDURING MENTORSHIP—THE PROFESSOR, THE NAVY CAPTAIN, AND THE PRIEST

I had many wonderful influences at The Citadel as well as my first encounter with mentorship. Certainly, the leadership within the cadet corps was ever present, but those were young men trying their hand at leadership for the first time in most cases. I had professors who were engaging and often possessed a wry sense of humor, and they served as seasoned mentors. There was my German professor, hailing from Hungary, who admonished me publicly for poor German (I have since engaged in self-study to improve). I also recall fondly my business law professor who taught contract law so well I retained many of the lessons through my contract management time in the Navy.

And who could forget my English professor who could recite the most beautiful classical poetry and prose from memory followed by an expletive-laced dressing down if he caught you not paying attention—his barracks nickname was "trashmouth." Three gentlemen stood out while at The Citadel, and most of the exposure I had to these men was during my final two years of study. They were a professor, a Navy captain, and a priest.

The professor, we'll call him Dr. B, was an economics professor who taught micro and macro-economics, monetary policy, the nature of market forces, the ideas of Smith, Keynes and Friedman, and the then-current application of Reaganomics. He was also a fellow Episcopalian, so we interacted outside class with discussions of liturgy, Anglican music, national church policies and politics, and so on.

Dr. B recognized I was pretty well-versed in the machinations of the church, and he also observed I took a hiatus from Episcopal services in Charleston during my first two and a half years at school (although I attended my home church regularly when I returned to Kentucky on furloughs). Late in my junior year, he advised me that The Citadel's long-standing St. Alban's Episcopal Chapel was going to have its final service in Bond Hall before being moved to the north transept of the school's main religious building—Summerall Chapel.

He chided that as a good Episcopalian in a city well represented by the denomination—and as a cadet in a school with six Episcopal alumni bishops in our history—I would be remiss if I did not attend. I agreed and attended. Dr. B was on hand with other cadets and administrators including a grizzled old retired Navy captain (we will call him Captain C) who was also a professor under whom I had not the pleasure of taking a class. The service concluded, and as I departed across the parade ground toward Murray Barracks, I heard from behind the booming voice of the Navy captain: "Mr. Palmer!"

The captain was head of the history department and an academic advisor to St. Alban's Chapel. Captain C was a retired reservist from the Deep South. He had exceedingly high standards of gentlemanly deportment and was quick to make corrections. One of his charges to cadets was to always carry two handkerchiefs (we were required to carry only one). "One is for you, and one is for an occasion in which a lady may require a gentleman's unsullied handkerchief."

Nineteenth-century lessons in gentlemanly behavior aside, barracks rumors abounded that he was once married but only for a short time because of his reputed curmudgeonry. He had a house on East Bay Street with old carriage spaces on the bottom floor converted to apartments he rented out to cadets attending summer school. Summer school students attended class in civilian clothes along with non-cadet students, and they could live off campus during the short-term while all other cadets were on furlough or summer ROTC training. Even so, Captain C conducted weekly inspections for order in the rooms he rented to the summer school cadets in Charleston. He was senior warden (highest elected board member) for one of the Charleston cathedrals and offered a generous Sunday lunch after church at his home to a variety of churchgoers and cadets. He was always teaching—always.

At his call I approached Captain C. I saluted and said, "Yes, sir?" He stated I looked as though I knew what I doing in the chapel service. I confessed I was a cradle Episcopalian. He asked why I was derelict in my religious duties over the past two years by not attending services regularly. I began to answer, and he cut me off saying, "The only acceptable answer is one you should have learned as a knob: 'No excuse, Sir.'" I responded: "No excuse, Sir." He assigned penance and stated I was now on the St. Alban's Chapel vestry (governing body). I stated I wasn't aware elections had occurred. Again, he cut me off and said, "As a new vestry member, you will attend Sunday lunch at my home, and we will discuss your duties for your senior year." To make a long story short, I was assigned to canvas all cadets who listed "Episcopal" as their faith and encourage them to attend St. Alban's Chapel services occurring conveniently on Monday evenings. They were led by the campus Episcopal priest, Father R.

Mom, Dad, Brooks, our kids, and I witnessed our son's baptism officiated by Father R at The Citadel's Summerall Chapel

Father R was a priest in the twilight of his career assigned as The Citadel's Episcopal chaplain. In his seventies, he offered counseling, a kind ear, an air-conditioned lounge with TV and soft chairs (our barracks rooms had no A/C back then), and popcorn and sodas after Monday evening services. He was the quintessential servant-priest and a gentleman to the core. Kindness radiated from him, and I grew to relish our discussions in his office. The first Episcopal service to which I took my girlfriend and future wife was the installation service of the new St. Alban's Chapel the fall of my senior year.

Fast-forward a few years. As a graduate and young Navy lieutenant, I had a notion to attend law school. Captain C wrote a scintillating letter on my behalf combined with good grades and a strong LSAT, and I was accepted. I did not attend; rather, I stayed in the Navy for a career. Still Captain C was always available for advice to this young graduate and fellow Naval officer. A few years later, I was a proud father of two children. My youngest child was born a few months before football season, and we went to Charleston to combine a football weekend with his baptism—in St. Alban's Episcopal Chapel—officiated by Father R.

I kept up with my trio of mentors, and over time Father R and Captain C were called home to be with the Lord. Only Dr. B remains. Some years later, our St. Alban's baptized son was in high school and had sights on attending The Citadel. Dr. B guided us through the admissions process and kept a distant eye on our boy as he navigated his own knob year, fourth-class system, and academic challenges throughout his time in Charleston.

A commencement tradition at our school, a graduate-parent of a graduating senior is permitted to sit on the dais and, at the appropriate time, present his child's diploma along side the college president. I traveled to Charleston, suited-up in my Service Dress Blues for the ceremony, and who did I see backstage before the procession? It was Dr. B, dressed in full academic regalia and now serving as provost. We swapped some old stories and took photos. I learned many lessons at The Citadel; however, it could be the best lesson imparted was a reinforcement of an enduring premise from our farm years—relationships matter.

Dr. B and I were reunited backstage before my son graduated from The Citadel in 2014.

EMBRACING ADVERSITY

As a final reflection, The Citadel touts itself as a leadership laboratory, and there are certainly important formative lessons taught in Charleston. For me, it was more of a perseverance laboratory. The Citadel follows the well-worn military school path of a plebe or fourth-class system affording participants an opportunity to accrue valuable "reps" and "sets" in overcoming adversity. The imposition of artificial hardship gets progressively difficult to build greater skills and confidence. The military school experience serves as a figurative "vaccination" against future fear of taking on tough challenges. Fight rather than flight is cemented into the graduates. For me it served as a natural extension from my farm foundation where as a child I often had to problem-solve things like broken equipment or missing livestock on my own.

Such adversarial environments appear to be more and more rare in the twenty-first century. Modern parents seek to shield their children from all adversity—to their detriment in my opinion. Today, too many children are rewarded for simply passing through childhood in unremarkable fashion. A premium is placed upon protection of feelings to the exclusion of gaining experience navigating adversity that makes for stronger adults. I believe parents, teachers, and mentors should encourage courageous endeavors in school, sports, hobbies, and employment—trial and error, trial and success. Most men and women value their hard-earned accomplishments over transient gifts. To strive and achieve makes one appreciate the strife and achievement. Embrace adversity and the thrill of meeting the challenge. Perseverance is still a valuable character trait—even today.

CHAPTER 6

U.S. NAVY—BACKGROUND

I commissioned into the Navy as an Ensign in the Supply Corps on my date of college graduation. The Supply Corps serves as the business managers of the fleet, and it is an operationally focused staff corps in the Navy—assigned to SEAL teams, submarines, and everything in between. Its motto is "Ready for Sea"—apropos as the formative years for nearly all Supply Corps officers are spent assigned to ships, squadrons, special warfare units, and explosive ordnance commands.

After six months at the Supply Corps Basic Qualification Course (BQC) in Athens, Georgia, I was assigned to an amphibious assault ship and participated in Operations Desert Shield and Desert Storm. I served on three other ships—a small guided missile frigate and two nuclear-powered aircraft carriers totaling nearly nine years of duty at sea, and it is in the arduous underway environment where many of the Navy's best leadership lessons are taught and learned.

With future wife Brooks at my orders reading party in 1988

After ten years of service, the Navy sent me to the Naval Postgraduate School in Monterey, California, for a Master's of Science in Systems Management with a focus on Acquisition and Contract Management. For the next twenty years, I alternated between contract management tours, sea duty, policy positions, and a fantastic honor and challenge: command over four shore-based units. Thirty-two years of service gave me the opportunity to experience and observe leadership challenges at the tactical, operational, and strategic levels. My tours ashore at operational staff and logistics commands also afforded me insight into the career paths of civil servants, and commercial strategic alliances exposed me to corporate executives as we partnered to support the warfighter. There was a perpetual challenge to continue my learning and master concepts of increased complexity. Self-awareness and continuous improvement are fundamental to the growth and development of Naval officers, and these officers must remain agile and open to learning as assignments evolve from afloat military units to multifaceted shore commands.

CHAPTER 7

NAVY JUNIOR OFFICER (JO)– THE FIRST TEN YEARS

VALUE AND HARMONY

"Why should I hire you?" That is the question all mentors advise job seekers to have suitcased before an interview. It is equally applicable to military officers although the hiring process is different. What do senior officers evaluating potential junior officers or businesses evaluating college graduates want? Is it acumen, drive, willingness to sacrifice, connections, writing ability, speaking ability, technological savvy, character, diversity, or a collegial nature? In all likelihood a prospective employer will be impressed by some combination of the many talents one can bring to the table. Nevertheless, for entry-level professionals, the equation can all boil down to two elements: value and harmony.

Do you add value and harmony? Value in the military is a simple matter of bringing to bear the skills and effort to advance the command's pursuit of mission. Most often, the mission is some form of combat lethality or support of units deployed and engaged in combat. In the corporate world, value comes down to dollars and cents. It is the combination of technical or professional skills applied appropriately to increase company revenue or reduce cost at a level greater than the cost of your employment. Is the company making or losing money as result of your employment? Understanding one's value permits professionals to be better negotiators of compensation. An employee oblivious to their value added to the company is likely to undersell or over-demand.

Harmony is much a more subjective additive to the value proposition. Do you have a positive attitude? Do you sacrifice to advance the team, division, or corporate goals? Are you indifferent about receiving individual credit to the ultimate benefit of the team? Do you have good character? Do you understand the work/life balance required to keep your family and friends supporting your career?

Conversely, do you carry baggage to the work place? Are you a distraction? Do you bring politics, religion, or money into workplace communications? Are you afraid of challenges? Are you self-absorbed at the expense of the team, division, or corporate goals? Are you a member from the legions of the self-defeated—victims who nurse invisible wounds inflicted by the idealism of academia? Harmony is delicate, but it is a critical counterbalance to the value you bring.

LT(jg) Palmer carrying a gas mask—onboard USS *Guam* (LPH 9) transiting the Suez Canal to Operations Desert Shield and Desert Storm in 1990

Remember, the military unit or corporate workplace is also a place of competition; winners and losers will reveal themselves in how they balance the need to shine individually with the needs of the team. One might be tempted to look only to self-promotion as a primary function—the lone wolf model. But the fact of the matter is, with few exceptions, you will be a member of a team where the fortunes of the individual membership stand upon the achievements of the greater team. An officer or employee will find little success, sometimes limited longevity, if they bring only one or none of these elements to the table—value and harmony.

YOU'RE IN THE BUSINESS OF FOLLOWING ORDERS

The military tries to simplify things for new entrants. Boot camp or officer training seems ridiculous with the high volume, focus on minute details, and pressurized situations, but the purpose is to introduce a small number of simple functions a youngster can master to build a foundation for confidence and future learning. Once the basic training or qualification courses are complete, junior officers have a simple mission. As I have told many junior enlisted and Naval officers (ensigns): "You're in the business of following orders." It is all about execution and effort. Demonstrate your worth and dedication by handling the basics and establishing mastery of your craft. Intelligence and innovation are appreciated, but only if you're covering the basics and doing your part to advance the interests of the squad/division/team and the greater unit.

This is the apprentice phase where a new entrant, junior officer, law firm associate, first time/first level supervisor "make their bones" through brute force and effort. You should be tired at the end of the workday, and this should force you to align work and play and family relationships to keep things in balance. Cover the basics at work and at home, and you'll be entrusted with more responsibility.

TIME MANAGEMENT

In 1988, I was an ensign in the Navy Supply Corps School's Basic Qualification Course in wonderful Athens, Georgia. They showed us a hokey time management film from the 70s entitled *Time of Your Life* narrated by James Whitmore. It was based on the book *How to Get Control of Your Time and Your Life* by Alan Lakein. This time management tool kit was exceedingly simple and foundational for me in how I managed my time throughout my Navy career. It is an easy process of listing all required tasks and asking: "What is the best use of my time now?" Tasks are broken down by importance and/or immediacy under an alphabetic priority system (A, B, C). A secondary numerical priority system is applied for each A, B, and C (e.g., A1, A2, A3, B1, C1, C2, etc.). Once prioritized, you estimate the time required for each task, overlay it on your calendar, start with A1 and then A2 and work your way as far into Bs and Cs as possible. The next day, strike out the completed tasks, add new tasks to the unfinished old tasks, reevaluate and reorder, and repeat the prioritized calendar execution. One of the most important things from this tutorial was to "write it down."[9]

WRITTEN ARTIFACTS AND ENABLERS

According to multiple time management experts, written goals are much more likely to be addressed and accomplished than goals existing only in the mind. I have maintained logbooks bound and permanent for thirty-two years where I did a daily prioritized "to do" list and calendar. I also recorded notes from meetings, important contacts, phone numbers, etc. Each logbook covers approximately six months, so I have several dozen spanning three decades. Although a couple have been lost to military moves, the majority exist in my library. I have them for reference, background, and proof of execution of meetings, decisions, and events.

I have, on dozens of occasions, referred back several books to refresh my memory on meeting discussions and actions or to look up a past contact that may be of use in the present. I also prefer written logs to typed records kept digitally on computer hard drives or cloud storage. Computer files are easily manipulated after the fact and such manipulations can be difficult to detect. Conversely, written logs with dated pages, ink color, handwriting style, and little spare surface area on the page (to falsify late-entries) hold more veracity in my experience.

A secondary benefit is many bosses appreciate young professionals who take notes in meetings. In fact, some insist on it. I remember well the admonishment from a salty Navy captain: "If you ain't writing, you ain't listening." Finally, writing helps me reinforce the knowledge and events in my memory more so than typing notes on a computer for future reference or relying upon unsupported recollection.

Another key enabler is a swiveling white board with a ninety-day calendar on one side and a "wolf board" on the other. The ninety-day calendar is self-explanatory, but I will point out this twentieth-century manual process is in fact superior to twenty-first-century electronic calendars for group alignment. Computers and smart phone calendars are typically used by individuals to view only a small square of time (an hour or day) to check for availability and conflicts. They are also seldom used or useful to groups examining time-phased challenges. A big ninety-day calendar on a white board in the frequent view of key staff at meetings synergizes all efforts, gives situational awareness of multiple competing projects, and allows all people to see all tasks to get on the same page.

The opposite side of the swiveling whiteboard is the "wolf board," and it lists the hottest tasks or "wolves closest to the sled" to focus the attention for every staff member. It can be a simple list or a series of lists for each staff directorate. It is most effective when you use a priority system similar to Lakein's model (A1, A2, B1, C1) to determine what the wolves are and the order of importance. Again, the staff meeting should be informed by the calendar and wolf board; these two enablers serve to align the efforts of all concerned.

There is also the added benefit of the boards providing "pop in" protection to deal with people senior to you dropping by your office or work area unannounced to check on your operations. This has happened dozens of times for me on ships and ashore, and it is always good to be able to control the conversation coolly and calmly with the help of the calendar and wolf board. It also reinforces the impression to bosses, coworkers, subordinates, and observers that you have your act together—not a bad perception to cultivate. Remember, as a young professional or junior officer, you're in the business of following orders and executing an array of rapidly unfolding tasks as you "make your bones." It is hard to keep it under control and organized when under pressure, so write it down.

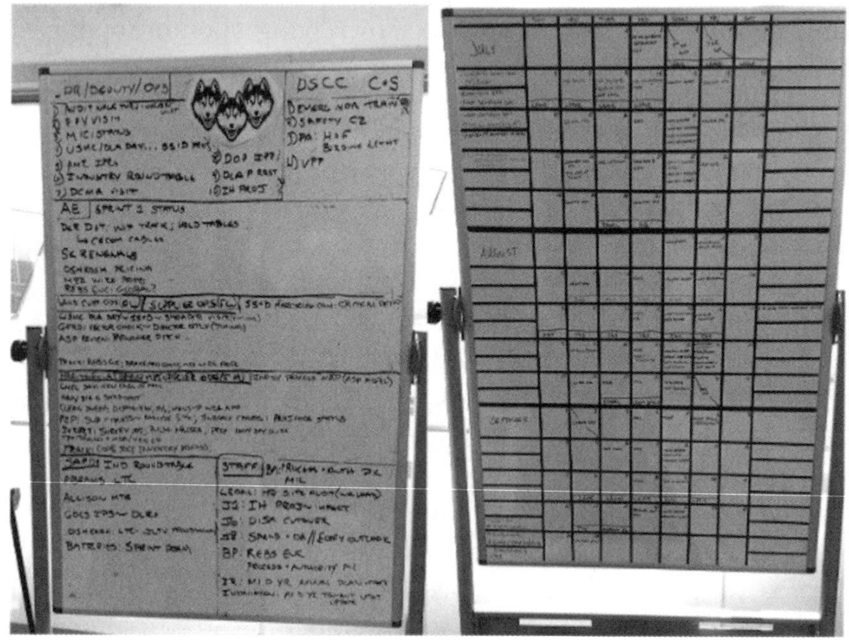

"Wolf board" and ninety-day calendar from weekly staff meeting—summer 2019

PLANNING AND COMMUNICATIONS

Planning—is a "must-have" and fundamental to nearly all organizations. Planning and communications are two all-important complementary skills at all levels of operations, but they're especially important to junior officers/young professionals who are tackling new challenges that change daily. Regarding planning: I am not referring to the formal operational and logistics planning taught in the war colleges. I am addressing the simple process of understanding the sequence of events that must occur to carry off the team, unit, or corporate mission; the role you play; and the actions you must complete to contribute to success as you ultimately add value.

My planning advice to junior officers was simple. You must be self-aware about the activity inside and outside your job area. You have to know the major unit goals, understand your team's necessary contributions, put the milestones for which you are responsible on long and short-range calendars, and build the sub-tasks to achieve the milestones.

A litmus test for poor planning was expressed as follows: "If you arrive at work and you are 'surprised' by your own calendar, you are failing the most basic planning function of having a handle on today's work." If you've lost situational awareness on today, there will be little confidence you have tomorrow, next month, next quarter, next year planned appropriately. The plans you derive may be simply for your use to keep your efforts optimal, but more likely they will involve coworkers and subordinates, and that is where the key second ingredient is brought to bear—communications.

Communications—my definition: "Communications are the root of all evil when you don't have enough, and they cure all ills when you apply more." Communications are really the key to any high-performing organization both formally planned and ad hoc. Formal communications are extremely important for establishing the schedule for transmitting or receiving messages. In the military, we call it the "battle rhythm." More formally, joint doctrine (across services) identifies this as boards, bureaus, centers, cells, and working groups (B2C2WGs).[10] These are the daily, weekly, monthly, quarterly, etc. leadership, staff, and project meetings planned and occurring with some type of minutes and upline reporting.

Battle rhythm communications are important as they establish an expectation as to when one will receive and/or be able to deliver communications. Ad hoc communications are one-on-one communications required to execute the day's duties. The best "as required" communications are ones using the minimal richness or complexity of media to carry off the message (e.g., email, phonecon, face-to-face, VTC, etc.). The selection of media is important. I advised junior officers that email is good for routine communications; however, if the issue is or could be contentious, you're better served with a richer medium (phonecon or face-to-face). Hearing/seeing the recipient tells you if your potentially contentious message is being received in the spirit you intend; consequently, you can make on-the-spot adjustments. A raised eyebrow, change in voice tone, or pregnant pause can signal if you're reaching the desired effect or not. More than a few relationships have been damaged by misinterpreted emails, and as we will see: relationships go from important to all-important as one progresses in seniority.

EMAILS WITH BIAS

A note about emails and writing in general: use bottom-line-writing incorporating the bottom line up front (BLUF).[11] This is a lesson I learned while pursuing a master's degree at Naval Postgraduate School in Monterey, California. Time is too precious for a four-page, twelve-paragraph email with the "money statement" buried surreptitiously in the tenth paragraph on the third page. No one has time for that.

My instructions at the onset of every command were that unless the email is four lines or fewer—use BIAS (BLUF, issue, action, suspense). In addition to brevity, the BIAS format also often conveys the essential elements for effective or SMART delegation (specific, measurable, achievable, relevant, and time-bound). Sometimes my first email to the new team would be in the BIAS format—explaining the design as outlined below:

- BLUF: The purpose of this email is to highlight the method of complex email communications we will employ until further notice. It incorporates categories of BIAS: BLUF (bottom line up front), issue(s), action(s), and suspense.
- Issues:
    - We have no time for excessive and undisciplined blather in our communications.
    - We require an orderly format for complex email communications (emails in excess of four lines not including salutation and signature blocks).

- The BIAS system will be utilized until further notice.
- Action: Emulate this email on all future complex emails.
- Suspense: Execute immediately.

******

- Background: You may add a "background" section if you have extra information, heavily detailed, technical, or cover-your-backside (CYA) items you feel compelled to include in the email. You may do so after the "suspense" portion of the BIAS format. Please understand, some people will neither read nor derive benefit from items you place in background, but it is an option open to you if you feel so compelled.

NOTE: After issuing the instructive email, if I received a pages-long tome not in keeping with bottom-line (BIAS) email guidance, I would return it to the sender by "reply" with the BIAS email attached and direct them politely to reformat their email.

KNOW YOUR BUSINESS—KNOW THE BUSINESS

KYB-KTB. If you're in the business of following orders—execution, as it were—you need to know the "blocking and tackling" of the basic work for which you and your team are responsible. This requires a combination of formal training, process examination, and on-the-job training (OJT). Knowing your business (KYB) is aligned closely with knowing your people, their roles and responsibilities, their level of training, and any gaps in personnel and training that exist. The foundation for your business is also the governing processes and policies as well as assigned plant and equipment. These are translated into standard operating procedures and checklists that must be followed as well as the upper and lower limits (redlines) put in place to indicate when your team is operating or producing a product out of tolerance. Process examination will be critical for (1) process compliance and ultimately (2) process improvement, but you must understand the as-is to be able to envision and achieve the "to be." Knowing your business is the first step and soon gives way to "knowing the business"—KTB.

KTB is a function of understanding the things impacting your team's performance but are not within your direct control. These may be the functions of other teams and their leaders such as comptrollers, elements in the process chain before and after your team plies their work, etc. This is a really good time to begin developing your skills of self-awareness and situational awareness as these particular proficiencies will increase in importance as you grow more senior. Understanding the entire process allows you to add value outside the confines of your sphere of influence (or as some say in the military—"outside your wire").

Understanding more about the business allows you to (1) effectively communicate the resource needs of your team, (2) guard against inaccurate assertions about your team's performance by a cohort or superior, (3) speak the all-important "budgetese" to understand limits and make a play for increased support, and (4) understand the balance among the command or corporate interests that must be struck for the greater team to win. Knowing your business/knowing the business are fundamental to understanding "trade-off" which is a survival skill for moving "into the gray" spaces discussed later in this book. But for now: "KYB-KTB."

KNOW THE MISSION—IF YOU CAN'T SEE IT, YOU CAN'T HIT IT

Identifying with your people, knowing your business, and the business outside your wire provides the junior officer/new entrant professional the foundation to adequately support the mission of the unit or company. It is important to be mission minded. To borrow a baseball analogy: "If you can't see it, you can't hit it." Mission awareness operates much the same way in that a leader simply functioning within the myopia of his or her team dynamics is often not effectively doing their part to support the greater objectives. The mission should be stated in the company literature, on walls, bulletin boards, etc. From a military perspective, we can see supporting connectivity throughout the chain of command informed by a president's national defense strategy, down through the national military strategy, various echelons of command, to the unit level. Corporate, business unit, or directorship missions should have similar linkage. Leaders should remain flexible, because the arrival of a new personality (president, secretary, commanding officer, CEO, COO) can drive mission review and revision that could change the team requirements. In this regard, another baseball analogy applies: "Be ready for the 'changeup.'"

TODAY'S WORK TODAY

Today's work today—in the world of entry-level, high-volume execution—simply means you have to stay on top of the work. Carryover work (either production or administrative) can bog down an operation. I always advised the team to complete "today's work today" without fail and to plan for the contingency it could require overtime to do so. Ideally, through proper planning, there should be ample opportunity to complete today's work during working hours. Occasionally, the chaotic nature of tactical work drives a push and pull of priorities possibly resulting in incomplete work at the end of the day. To leave it for afterhours duty personnel (watchstanders—military) or to the newly arrived corporate teammates (sucks to be you) will result in most cases in slipshod and error-filled work. A "just get it done" attitude will creep in and erode both quality and morale. Teamwork means sometimes the team has to adapt and overcome—together. Regardless, "today's work today" is a good rule to live by.

ETHICS ARE NON-NEGOTIABLE—THE KIDS ARE WATCHING

An organization must rest upon a solid ethical foundation. Most organizations at least make the pretense of ethical standards. Become familiar immediately with the company ethics posture and redlines, and be prepared to reinforce them or promulgate your own redlines. This is important to establish a climate of good order and discipline. For some operations, the basics of "lie, cheat, and steal" are the redlines not to be crossed on peril of punishment or dismissal. There may be other redlines as they relate to behavior in the workplace (e.g., sexual harassment, hostile work environment, etc.). Catchphrases are often invoked: "Good, right, and honorable"—"guard the public trust as if it was your own money."

There should be institutional redlines bolstered by your standards. In the absence of institutional redlines, you must fill the gap. It is important to make clear to your team what you will and will not tolerate. If you are unfortunately assigned to a lax organization operating loosely with little deference to established policies and procedures, you would be well served to be the "by the book" entity in the group. Devil-may-care attitudes are fun but fleeting and often leave professional destruction (potentially reprimand or jail time) in their wake. Some leaders fall prey to the notion seniority grants them a pass on adherence to ethics—it doesn't. All leaders must remember, "the kids are watching." Wanton violations of ethics invariably result in lower-level imitators plying the same trade.

SHOOT STRAIGHT—BE A STAND-UP GUY/GAL

A straight shooter is an honest broker largely unconcerned with self-promotion—a purveyor of facts not feelings. Young leaders are tempted to try to advance quickly and sometimes cast an eye toward shortcuts to curry favor with senior officials. They occasionally jump headlong into the politics of situations without the experience to exercise forbearance. They can lose mission focus, and it impacts their team and the organization. When things start to go south, scared junior professionals are sometimes tempted to blame their subordinates for missteps rather than being a "stand-up guy or gal" and taking responsibility. Hypocrisy is a serious blow to a young professional's credibility. Leaders who have or appear to have self-interest prioritized at the expense of team-interest erode morale.

REMEMBER THE BASICS: ENERGY + FUNDAMENTAL PROFICIENCY = GOODWILL AND (AT TIMES) BENEFIT OF THE DOUBT

- Effort counts.
- Energy counts.
- Putting in the hours counts.
- Covering the basics counts.
- Paying your dues counts.

These exhibitions of energy are not the desired end state and sometimes not enough to counter failure to achieve the mission, but they are often taken into consideration. This consideration or benefit of the doubt can make a difference in your assessment by your superiors. When I was a student at Navy Supply Corps School, the school's CO used to say: "I'm gonna give you a lit stick of dynamite to take to your first ship." The inference was that upon graduation, we would be energized and educated to hit our first sea-duty assignments with maniacal enthusiasm.

When you display this enthusiasm, it balances the scales somewhat when you make a mistake. The thought process of the superior may be: "If this issue got the best of this 'energizer-bunny' of an officer, it would have gotten the best of anyone else." And, you might get a second chance. However, if you have in your record slothfulness, indifference, or a too-cool-for-school track record, your past performance will not balance the scales. Rather, the sub-optimal offerings will "tip the scales" out of your favor. Look at yourself through the eyes of your boss, and ask yourself if you like what you see. And remember, if you're going to make mistakes, make sure they are "mistakes of effort."

YOU GET WHAT YOU INSPECT, NOT WHAT YOU EXPECT—NOTHING SHOWS YOU CARE LIKE SHOWING UP

This time-tested inspect/expect precept is a close cousin to "meet your people in their spaces," and it is also a valued enabler to management-by-walking-around (MBWA). Bottom line—setting the standard is one thing, but holding teammates accountable is another. My roommate on my first ship (USS *Guam*) was the food service officer, and he was exceptional with this management technique. From galleys to storerooms to dining areas—he seemed to be everywhere as his team executed all-hours feeding of Marines and Sailors through the eight-month wartime deployment in Operations Desert Shield/Storm.

The lesson: As a junior officer or company first line supervisor, you must get out in the office spaces, warehouses, lower decks, magazines, and storerooms to observe operations and people in action. Knowledge among the workforce that you're liable to show up is good preventative medicine against slothful behavior, naps, video games during working hours, etc. Do not confuse this as micromanagement. As a junior (division) officer, platoon leader, or company first line supervisor, YOU ARE SUPPOSED TO KNOW what your people are doing. As you get more senior with an increased scope of responsibilities—especially if you are forced to practice distance-leadership—phrases such as "I was unaware" or "No one brought that to my attention" are sometimes understandable. But such is NOT the case for first tour officers and new entrant professionals.

"Nothing shows you care like showing up" is recognition that if you care enough to be on site—you actually care about the mission accomplishment and the conditions in which your teammates have to work. In my shipboard tours, I was often seen in storerooms, on flight decks, and aircraft elevators observing or participating in crane operations and material movement. Why? First, as a former farm kid, I liked hard work and observing people and machinery in action. Second, I was getting what I inspected. Third, the crew knew I was aware of their work conditions. If it was hot, cold, windy, rainy—I could ensure proper protections were taken. The "nothing shows you care like showing up" also extends to off-hours events such as coworker hospitalizations and injury recovery, special events, promotion ceremonies, recognition of big family events, knowledge of down times, etc. In moments of "glad and sad," nothing shows you care like showing up.

THE FIRST STORY IS NEVER THE STORY

At some point, you will receive an emergent report from a breathless subordinate that something is awry. There will be the temptation to charge into the fray and correct the issue as soon as possible. Certainly, there are situations where this is a necessity such as a shipboard fire, combat casualties, etc., but those are somewhat rare. More often, problems can be addressed with some degree of quick study, and this is important to avoid being whipsawed by fast but incomplete reports. There will be a temptation to run immediately to your boss and say, "We've got a problem!" However, as a leader, you have the responsibility to rapidly gather the facts, and it is this crossroad where "the first story is never the story" comes into play.

An admiral mentor of mine advised me before I reported to serve as the Supply Officer (senior logistician) on board the aircraft carrier *Harry S. Truman*: "The first story is always wrong." I changed the phraseology somewhat, but the message is the same. You must dig in quickly and find out the preponderance of the facts at a minimum to determine the appropriate initial actions and upline reporting. Why—because the first story is never the story, and the second story could be better, or worse, or overcome by events (OBE).

Start with the "five Ws" also known as "who, what, when, where, and why." You may also take quick counsel from your key employees/subordinates and colleagues to determine initial actions to stop or slow the suboptimal situation, and you should give decisive initial orders. Still—that is not the end. There is upline reporting required. If you approach your supervisor with the five Ws and informed recommendation(s), the reporting process will go better. You will also more likely receive better direction from your boss if you provide him/her a complete report.

Finally, there could be some type of after-action report (AAR) or inquiry if the misstep is serious. Embrace the AAR or inquiry. It will assist in determining the facts, required future process adjustments, and serve as a foundation if the disciplining of a team member is required. But remember—the underpinning is good solid facts, and those facts are seldom revealed sufficiently in the "first story."

PRAISE IN PUBLIC/CRITICIZE IN PRIVATE—ALWAYS LEAVE THEM WITH THEIR DIGNITY

While establishing and holding the line on ethical standards, process, policy, team goals, and unit goals, you will periodically encounter teammates who do not perform to standards either intentionally or unintentionally. The standards of firmness, fairness, and consistency apply to corrective measures such as on-the-spot corrections, counseling, and performance improvement plans. The age-old adage "praise in public/criticize in private" is a good rule of thumb as it permits the coworker(s) in question to maintain their dignity. But there are exceptions.

If "lie, cheat, steal" is in the mix, you may have to go publicly coercive. My additional (personal) redlines were insubordination or the public impugnment of another's dignity. If you observe a coworker being abused physically or sexually, ganged-up on, or otherwise humiliated; immediate and public action must be taken, and there must be no doubt in these situations where you stand. Additionally, if a female leader receives a "boys club" remark made at her expense, it must be challenged publicly and fervently by the female leader. She should not let a male in the room defend her as this only reinforces the "fairer sex" stereotype. She has to adjust the behavior by her own hand. Pain and discomfort (figuratively) are motivators to be certain; however, such methods should be used sparingly since frequent use erodes morale and rings hollow over time. I pride myself on keeping my cool as it is part of my natural disposition to handle all things with calm control; however, in the realm of protecting a teammate (even from other teammates)—I permit myself to raise my voice in those rare occasions.

Absent abuse or clear unit/corporate redline violations (lie, cheat, steal), I find public praise and private admonishment the "well-worn path" to follow. I also recommend serving up a PNP sandwich (positive-negative-positive). PNP is simple—start the counseling or on-the-spot correction with a positive aspect of the teammate's performance followed by the substandard areas. Corrective actions (potentially plans) may then be addressed finishing with yet another positive affirmation of the teammate's contributions and potential within the organization. This permits you to "leave them with their dignity" as you address shortcomings. In summary, unless abuse or ethical violations indicating fundamental character flaws have occurred, you always want to leave your supporting teammates with their dignity.

My second ship (a frigate) and first department head tour from 1994–1996—USS *Boone* (FFG-28) serving as ship's Supply Officer and helicopter control officer[12]

IT'S A MARATHON, NOT A SPRINT—PACE AND BALANCE

I have witnessed many young enlisted Sailors and commissioned Naval officers exhaust themselves in an attempt to get off to a good start. New officers and entrants must practice the "long game" as their new job is a multi-year endeavor and requires a marathon pace to make it to the finish line in good standing. There is a time and place to accelerate to a sprint—emergencies and combat come to mind, but in the day-to-day execution of your duties, you must apply consistent and persistent efforts. The marathon/sprint continuum is otherwise known as *pace*.

Balance is the other element in the mix. All work and no play make Johnny (and Janie) dull. Overwork also impacts the families of your teammates. There must be a balance of work, play, hobbies, and downtime to recharge batteries and enable the completion of the marathon with an occasional "sprint" as required. The balance must not teeter too much to work nor too much to play. A worker who is over-fixated on a hobby (such as vintage car restoration or following a sports team around the country) will permit work to suffer. Your team requires healthy and happy members and extended families.

Exigencies of work (deployments and deadlines) and family (births, deaths, family moves) will certainly require the scales to tip back and forth temporarily, and this must be accommodated. However, the scales should not tip too far, and there will have to be a complementary swing the other way to compensate and keep the individual and team in balance and on pace.

YOU'RE IN A COMPETITION—EVERYTHING HAPPENS FOR A REASON

As with most aspects of life, you are engaged in some form of competition, and this is certainly the case with your profession. You need to shine. You need to demonstrate your worth. The unit or company leadership needs to see you're adding value, and you should be a contributing member of the team. In the spirit of competition, you need to give a stringent individual effort with the goal of performing better or at least as good as the best junior performers in the organization. Remember however, this is all within the context of contributing to team success. A high-performer on a losing team is still a loser, but you can mitigate the loss by being the silver lining to the dark cloud that accompanies the unsuccessful endeavor or project.

Hopefully, someone will glean your work as the exception to the second-place finish or lost cause. The best course of action is to maintain the press, but just know there are only so many losses the unit/firm will accept before they see the hard driver on the hard luck team as part of the problem—not the solution. A bit player on a winning team will receive some recognition, although over time the value they are not adding will become apparent. A hard-driving ship's captain once taught us: "Everything happens for a reason," and this is certainly true.

You are in control of your actions and, to a great extent, the actions of your team. You need to make sure you are part of the reason for the successes achieved by the unit. Moreover, you should be part of the solution to problems that exist to include risk mitigation for failed endeavors. In the end it all comes back to the original premise. You must add value and harmony to optimize your prospects in any organization. Good luck and keep charging!

Deployed to the Mediterranean Sea and conning the ship during underway replenishment under the watchful eye of the ship's commanding officer—USS *Boone* (FFG-28)

CHAPTER 8

TALES FROM THE JO JUNGLE

ADDING VALUE—SET YOUR SIGHTS ON BECOMING INDISPENSABLE

This was a lesson taught at The Citadel by a retired Coast Guard captain teaching in the business department. The message was clear: an indispensable man or woman will always have a place in the organization. Upon arriving to my first ship, the amphibious assault ship USS *Guam* (LPH 9), we were moored in Rota, Spain, returning from a six-month deployment. I was an outsider. The crew was filled with the excitement of seeing family members after six months of separation, yet I left Philadelphia international airport only a few hours earlier. They would receive "stand down" or time-off privileges not extended to me. My time on the deployment consisted of only the two-week transit from Rota, Spain back to the United States.

I was the new guy, so I settled into my temporary position as officer in charge of the yet-to-be established technical library while I awaited rotation into a typical ensign position as disbursing officer—the officer in charge of pay to the crew, cash management, and bill paying for the ship. On the return trip, I worked to learn the ship and supply department and add some value.

Shortly after arrival in our U.S. homeport, we had a logistics assessment where we did not perform as well as we expected in a couple of areas of inspection. Consequently, there was a shake-up in the department. As I was new and not part of the sub-optimal assessment results, I was designated as "part of the solution" for the material (parts) portion of the evaluation. The department head assigned me as S-8 (material) officer with cognizance over ship's support storerooms (millions of dollars in inventory) plus some functions typically assigned to other divisions (aviation storerooms, customer service, procurement, and transportation, to name a few).

I essentially transitioned from temporary librarian where there was no library to an ensign holding down a handful of jobs typically entrusted to a collection of lieutenants (two ranks higher). Here was a daunting opportunity—a time to pay my dues and make myself indispensable.

With the help of a remarkable chief petty officer, we took our patchwork functions and Sailors and homogenized them into S-8 Division. We were going into a drydock for maintenance, so being in charge of material, procurement, services, and transportation meant nothing would come or go to the ship without coming under our cognizance.

We established a division motto I borrowed from The Citadel's November Company: "No Slack." Consequently, we were "S-8—No Slack," and the motto could be seen in our spaces, on our T-shirts, and carved into decorative tile on our decks—everywhere. We became known as THE division to see if you wanted anything done in the yards. We worked fourteen-to-sixteen hours a day and became the "indispensable division" in the department and on the ship with a hand in most of the successes and some of the failures during the shipyard period spanning six months.

We pressed hard, sometimes too hard and charged headlong into some procedural errors and stepped on some toes. Any mistakes we made were "mistakes of effort," and we did not repeat them. Fortunately, we learned as we went along and arrived at many more successes than failures. Equally important, we improved our processes and the accountability of our material in the storerooms. By the end of the shipyard period, our division was respected, and our department's reputation recovered nicely from the missteps we encountered during the post-deployment logistics assessment. Moreover, I was recognized as the leader of the indispensable S-8 Division and, by extension, an indispensable officer in the wardroom.

SHOW UP—MAKE YOUR BONES—MAKE A SPLASH

After returning from deployment and the stand down period, we entered a shipyard in Norfolk. During the *Guam*'s shipyard period, the ship was elevated in a dry dock, and most of the crew had to be berthed (housed) and fed ashore in temporary facilities. Another part of the supply department (food service division) was plagued by midnight burglars breaking into the temporary galley ashore (a galley is a Navy restaurant facility either on a ship, a berthing barge, or on a base). Every few nights, the morning food service watch section reported to the galley at 3:30 a.m. to find the locks broken, door kicked in, food pilfered, and a mess left within the food services spaces.

Once every three days, I was required to stay on board the ship overnight as the duty supply officer (overnight representative of the department head who was a Navy commander). In my capacity as duty department head, I devised the idea of making a pallet upon which to sleep in a darkened corner just out of sight of the galley's locked door. I figured in two or three duty nights, I would be able to observe or potentially intervene in one of the burglaries. I asked the ship's security officer and he grumbled, "Sure, Ensign—give it a try, but don't come crying to me if you get hurt." The department head (supply officer) issued the okay to perform the after-hours surveillance. I didn't have to wait long.

On my first night of staking out the galley, I awoke at 2:00 a.m. to banging on the door. It was a man in civilian clothes kicking in the door. I moved in out of the dark and apprehended the culprit who turned out to be one of our Sailors, drunk and just back from liberty on the town. I nabbed him, took his ID, ordered him to his berthing and awoke the duty security officer to take over.

The next morning, my supply officer at the department head meeting, said "In one night, my new ensign cracked the rash of theft and burglary that the security department has been failing to stop for weeks." There were no more attempted break-ins at the galley, and the word spread on board all the way to the ship's captain. My reputation shifted from one of many anonymously capable officers to an officer who could make things happen. I made a splash.

It is important to note, there was risk in this strategy. In retrospect, I had no idea if the thieves would be one person or a half dozen. What if they turned on me? I liked my chances as I was still in Citadel shape, but I could have been injured or worse. As it stood, it worked, and it put me in the upper echelon of the ship's junior officers in the minds of the commanding officer (ship's captain), executive officer (second in command), and my department head (supply officer).

WHEN YOU LEAST EXPECT IT, EXPECT IT!—BE READY TO ADAPT

There were many noteworthy achievements for the Sailors and embarked Marines of USS *Guam* highlighted by a no-notice deployment to participate in Operations Desert Shield and Desert Storm. In August 1990, we got underway quickly on short notice from another period in the shipyards. In a little over one week, we reassembled our ship's systems and deployed without workups accompanied by the embarked Marines with whom we had never operated. We took an asymmetric complement or aircraft (all CH-46 helicopters instead of a mix of Marine Corps aircraft for which our storerooms were loaded). I was reassigned from S-8 Division, to S-6 Division responsible for aviation support of the Marine Corps helicopters. I was blessed to have an ace first class petty officer to help me run the division. We deployed and served admirably in Operations Desert Shield, Eastern Exit, and Desert Storm in that order.

During Desert Storm (Gulf War), the enemy forces were massed in Kuwait to repel an amphibious invasion from the sea. As part of the amphibious task force, we were prepared to approach and launch our Marines ashore from the east. However, in the spirit of Operation Overlord's "Pas de Calais," the strategy was modified for us to launch empty aircraft as a feint to convince the enemy we were assaulting from the sea—holding them in their entrenched positions so the Allied coalition ground forces could attack and defeat them from the south and west.[13]

The amphibious feint worked as designed, but it was not without risk. During our operations in the western Persian Gulf, we had to transit mined waters. Two ships hit mines. *Guam* did not. Still, USS *Guam* was one of several ships' crews who received the combat action ribbon for the operations conducted in mined waters.[14] The events of the eight-month deployment taught us the best-laid plans are rapidly torn asunder when the pressures of war are exerted on the nation and Navy. In the macro sense, things changed very fast as we deployed, trained, participated in the Gulf War, conducted a non-combat evacuation operation (NEO) rescue of civilians from Somalia (discussed later), and successfully returned home.

WHEN YOU LEAST EXPECT IT, EXPECT IT! KNOW YOUR SURROUNDINGS—MACRO-TO-MICRO

At the unit level onboard *Guam*, we encountered many challenges in the aviation support division. We had a great Navy/Marine Corps team in the division, but unpredictability and agility were a daily norm. One day during a short logistics port visit at Jebel Ali (near Dubai in the United Arab Emirates), we had an aircraft engine shipped from the United States to a nearby foreign air base in Abu Dhabi where the U.S. Air Force had a presence.

I had the task of taking a hired 2½-ton truck and local national driver to the other emirate to pick up the engine and return to the ship. My driver, named Majid, spoke very little English, and we communicated as well as we could. We drove through the barren spaces between Dubai and Abu Dhabi. Even in the pre–9/11 environment, the little voice in the back of my head said my buddy Majid could drive me into a camp of bad guys, and I would have no recourse until it was too late.

I was in uniform, but unarmed. We were on the road from a place at which I only arrived a short while ago, to a place I had never been, with signs along the roadway I could not read. I made a mental note to never again let Lieutenant (junior grade) Palmer be so tactically blind and at the mercy of factors outside my control.

We made it safely to the Abu Dhabi airbase guarded by local military members. We stopped at the inspection station outside the gate. The guards asked Majid a few questions in Arabic, and whatever he said was the wrong answer as the inquisitor pulled him from the truck cab, threw him facedown on the hot road surface and pointed an automatic weapon at him while the rest of the armed detail approached my side of the truck. I slowly raised my hands, so they could view them. Another uniformed official came to my door and in good English asked for my identification and any paperwork. I gave him my ID and transfer paperwork for the aircraft engine. He told me I could proceed, but without Majid—he was not permitted on the base.

Fortunately, my farm kid experience made driving the large truck a snap. I drove on base, followed the directions given to me by the gate guard, and had my aircraft engine in about thirty minutes. As I was driving out of the base, I wondered what happened to Majid. Would he even be at the gate as I departed? How would I get back to Dubai? I was intent on getting off the base and back to the ship quickly, but something stopped me. I saw the U.S. Air Force detachment having a cookout. I hadn't had a grilled burger outside of the sliders on the ship in about four months.

I stopped and bought burgers for me, a ration for Majid in case he was still outside the base, and I also obtained a roadmap from the USAF airmen in case I had to find my way back without Majid. As it turns out, Majid, was exactly where I left him—laying on the ground guarded by an armed Emirati military serviceman. I pulled up, he wiped the gravel and sweat off his face, happily took the hamburgers and sodas, and we were off.

Lessons learned from this deployment and trip were plentiful. In a macro perspective (ship's schedule, operational assignment, and associated new daily challenges), the pendulum swings of change are out of our control, but we must be agile and able to adapt and perform. From a micro-perspective, I resolved to have full control and situational awareness in foreign countries from then on. I insisted upon familiarization briefs, security concerns, road maps, emergency phone numbers, and cell or satellite phones.

Whenever a trip to a foreign country was predictable, I learned two dozen basic phrases starting with "I am an American." "I don't speak _____ very well." "Where is _____?" "How can I _____?" and a few others including getting directions, food ordering, please and thank you. This paid huge dividends throughout the remainder of my career including operations on three other ships and my three commands with detachments in over a dozen countries. I became known as an officer who was well prepared, looking ahead, and who could function on the ground overseas because I was somewhat multilingual. This perception was not really true regarding my linguistic ability, but I was basic phrase functional.

FIXING A HARD-LUCK OPERATION—"IT'S NOT THE ONE THING, IT'S THE EVERYTHING"

As outlined previously, my second ship was a guided missile frigate (USS *Boone* (FFG-28)) homeported in Mayport, Florida. It was a tale of two commanding officers—both of them very good. The first CO arrived several months before I did. It was a hard-luck ship that failed multiple inspections to the point the homeport joke was we weren't even certified to hold colors (raise and lower the flag in the morning and evening). The CO recognized the disfunction and drove the crew hard and the officers harder. He implemented the apropos priority system of "Ship, Shipmate, Self." We worked sixteen-plus-hour days routinely including weekends as necessary. It was tough on the crew and tough on our families, but the ship had to be brought to standards.

I learned two things from this ship's captain. First, there are times when you have to "out-tough" a situation and sometimes "shock" a poor performing team onto a path of improvement. Not every leader can do this, but those who can prove invaluable in crisis. Second, when leading a complex operation, the root cause of your situation is seldom a single significant factor that needs to be corrected to bring the entire ship on-line. We were broken across the board—every department—every division, and my operation (supply department) was no exception.

I saw the captain exert herculean efforts to bring all substandard aspects to heel. It was then I coined a descriptive: "It's not the one thing, it's the *everything*." The CO led simultaneously the correction in the ship's operations, maintenance, training, tactics, morale, race relations, family support, and the officers "owning" the outcomes of their charges. We became proficient by the time we changed COs, and that was no small task.

Our second CO took the newly proficient ship, applied long-standing Navy standards and procedures, aligned our efforts to upcoming deployments, trained us to a razor's edge, and we thrived. After the pains of "fixing" the ship, the follow-on work-ups and deployment were a joy to execute. As we continued to improve, he loosened the reins appropriately so we could run like thoroughbreds as we performed in the fleet. In short, under our second CO, we normalized, standardized, put in the reps and sets, and crushed work-ups and deployments.

My view from "the tower" when serving as helicopter control officer on board the guided missile frigate USS *Boone* (FFG-28)

In the span of two COs, we went from a ship unable to get underway for pre-deployment preparations to a crew of highly successful deployers. The deployments included serving as a member of NATO forces in the Mediterranean to support ground operations in Bosnia, seizing narcotics in the Caribbean, and winning one of the Navy's Battle "E" awards for excellence (a fleet award presented annually to the best ships). What leadership lessons did I witness from *Boone*'s commanding officers? Two men, one ship, and a maximum effort led to the complete transformation of a vessel from a liability to a fleet asset worthy of emulation.

WATCH AND LEARN FROM YOUR MENTORS AT EVERY OPPORTUNITY

A wise admiral and mentor of mine used to tell his charges: "Good ideas from everywhere." This is unquestionably true. In the same light, good mentorship comes from everywhere as well. To be mentored, one has to have mentors. Mentorship is important because we stand on the shoulders of those who have gone before us. We would be foolish to ignore the lessons learned by our predecessors. My consistent advice to junior offices was to cultivate mentors at every stage of your career—during every tour. Enduring mentorship requires you to maintain frequent communications with your mentors over the years to keep the sage wisdom flowing. For me, I learned from subordinates and peers but more so from immediate superiors and every single commanding officer for whom I served—afloat and ashore. Some examples include: My Desert Storm department head (SUPPO) and commanding officer on board USS *Guam*. The CO went on to flag rank. Under these leaders, I learned how to be an execution-oriented junior officer, accountability, taking the long-view on challenges, and the primacy of proficiency in a warship's mission—making war.

On my second ship USS *Boone* (FFG-28), I was introduced to the "tin can" Navy on the guided missile frigate. I learned more about leadership, challenges, myself, my limits, and I witnessed dozens of lessons I would learn and take far into my career. I worked for two COs who voraciously attacked different problems and challenges at various times in the life of the ship. Both men were goal setters and more importantly goal achievers. I was blessed to be a part of a crew that navigated the crucible of drastic transformation.

My third and fourth ships were aircraft carriers—USS *George Washington* (CVN 73) and USS *Harry S. Truman* (CVN 75) where I worked with the cream of the crop in Navy talent, and we were afforded good manpower, support, and funding. I was privileged to serve with outstanding officers including lieutenant commander principal assistants who comprised some of the best seagoing performers I have ever witnessed.

My department head on the *George Washington* stands out as a superb leader encouraging us to "raise the bar," and he led us to those new heights. The carriers' COs were outstanding, especially when we responded to 9/11 by providing air cover to New York City immediately after the bombings, exacted some revenge during our wartime deployment to Operation Enduring Freedom, and deployed on short notice to deliver critical supplies to victims of Hurricane Katrina.

I was supported and mentored by some senior enlisted leaders who amaze me to this day—so much so I invited a handful from my USS *Washington* tour to join me on my final sea tour on board USS *Truman*. My final ship's CO was one of the finest gentlemen and leaders I have witnessed, and he eventually served at the rank of vice admiral as the Navy's inspector general. I witnessed great works and leadership in these high-performing ships.

In balance, I think one learns more at sea in the Navy than anywhere else, yet I was afforded outstanding mentoring ashore too. My first shore tour was as an instructor at Navy Supply Corps School where I joined a collection of the Navy's best Supply Corps officers charged with educating new ensigns for their entry into the fleet. We were commanded by a once-in-a-generation officer who went on to be a transformational leader in our community on the way to the rank of vice admiral.

My first tour after postgraduate school affiliated me with superb flag officer mentors. One of these admirals invited me to serve with him on multiple occasions. He rose to the pinnacle position of Chief of Supply Corps. Over the past quarter-century, he took me under his wing, provided astute wisdom, and he advises me to this day. There were many other magnificent leaders to whom I was exposed, and I believe myself to be a product of their mentorship and hard work.

I am fortunate to have been under the tutelage and to have served alongside so many "great Americans." To be sure, we were not perfect. I witnessed a few leaders who were mean spirited, self-promoting, or who had misaligned priorities—but they were rare. In addition, I was not perfect. I failed the standard sometimes, but I learned and improved. I absorbed equal measures of what to do as well as what not to do when my time to lead and command was placed before me. These mentors provided me my "tools in the tool kit" that proved fundamental to future success in the Navy and at multi-billion dollar joint operations ashore. We will cover more lessons learned—afloat and ashore—throughout the remainder of the book, but I think you will see the ever-present impact of good mentorship throughout.

CHAPTER 9

FIELD GRADE OFFICER/SENIOR OFFICER AND DIRECTOR

This section addresses the period of time in which an officer or professional transitions from subject matter expert (SME) to leader in a complex environment up to and including senior staff positions, command, major command, and civilian director positions. For the military, we are highlighting the period from ten to twenty-five years of commissioned service where one serves from paygrades O-4 through O-6 (major, lieutenant colonel, and colonel for Army, USMC, and USAF, and lieutenant commander, commander, and captain for Navy and USCG). For civil servants, the GS equivalents are GS-13, GS-14, and GS-15. For the corporate world, the loose equivalents might include mid-to-senior level positions up to but not including the C-suite.

LEADERSHIP—MILITARY VS. CIVILIAN

It is important to address the different leadership models that have arisen in the government between military and civil servants. Some do not realize the vast majority of the personnel serving within DoD are actually civil servants and not uniformed military. Military members typically spend their first few tours in operational units (ships, squadrons, rifle companies, etc.) where they master their craft

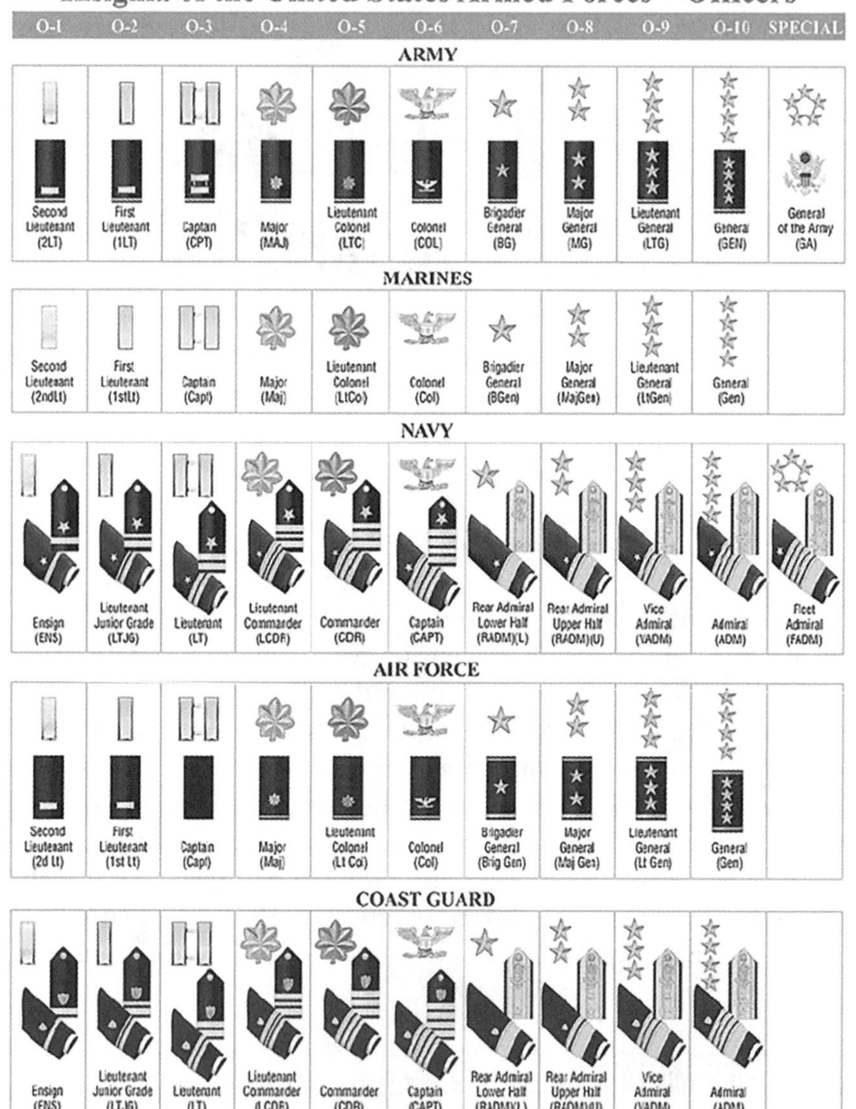

Armed Forces Rank Chart[15]

in a nearly all-military environment. However, as service members gain seniority and experience, they are detailed to higher echelon staffs referred to as "shore tours" in the Navy. These jobs are typically at commands providing some type of support to operational units. These shore tours are at commands manned to a large extent by civil servants.

Military officers spend about ten years as junior or "company grade" officers (paygrades O-1 through O-3—ranks 2nd lieutenant, 1st lieutenant, and captain for Army, USMC, and USAF, or ensign, lieutenant (junior grade), and lieutenant for Navy and USCG). As stated, military officers are charged with mastering their tactical craft in their first tours (e.g., flying, sailing, ground combat). Simultaneously, they are placed immediately into leadership roles. In the Army it may be platoon leader (platoon commander for USMC) and onboard ships; Naval officers are placed in charge of a "division"—typically a team of a dozen or so.

My examples were highlighted earlier in the book. I was placed in charge of S-8 or materiel division on board my first ship USS *Guam*. *Guam* was an amphibious assault ship charged with embarking Marines and placing them ashore in times of combat or a humanitarian assistance/disaster relief (HA/DR) situation. While still a junior officer, I encountered increased leadership challenges as a guided missile frigate supply officer (USS *Boone*) laying the foundation for two other sea tours as a logistician on aircraft carriers as a senior officer.

Junior officer leadership assignments are low level, they are supervised, and there is room to make mistakes without too much adverse impact on the unit or mission. By the time they promote to "field grade" officer (paygrade O-4), they are experienced flyers, ship drivers, or ground unit leaders, and they have ten years of practical leadership under their belts. In my experience, most aspiring leaders with fatal flaws in their performance or character are washed out before making field grade.

Conversely, civil servants are more often charged with continued mastering of their craft or becoming subject matter experts (SMEs) without as many early leadership opportunities. Frequently, civil servants are selected for leadership roles based on their SME proficiency such as contract management, engineering, budget management, analysis, item management, etc. As they enter their first leadership challenge, the newly minted civil servant leader is of fair seniority under the "general schedule" (GS) paygrade system.

Sometimes a civil servant will not be charged with leadership until they are a GS-13 (major or lieutenant commander equivalent). Remember, military majors and lieutenant commanders are riding a decade's worth of practical leadership experience by this time in their careers. This can be a real challenge for civil servants because they have relatively limited leadership experience, yet the mistakes made at the GS-13 level or above can bring significant impact to the organization. The penalty for first-time leadership mistakes is greater for civil servants by comparison. For military, it is baby steps and building blocks for a firm foundation of leadership. For civilians, it is leadership delayed with much more on the line.

Much is made about the high quality of military leadership, but in fact it is more likely the developmental process that is the root cause rather than some inherent natural ability accompanying the uniform. For military and civil servants, this is a beneficial area for self-awareness as they spend the majority of both types of careers in each other's company. For me, I served thirty-two years as a Naval officer in Navy and joint organizations. During my four sea tours, it was nearly an all-military club; however, over two-thirds of my career was spent ashore outnumbered and in the company of some amazing civil servants.

A final note to young military officers: leading military and civil servants requires slightly different skill sets given the presence or absence of the Uniform Code of Military Justice, HR policy for civil servants, time card adherence, different limits on hours of work, union representation, etc. If you apply an operational military lens to the leading of civil servants, you will fail. If you allow your military members to become de facto civilians-who-happen-to-wear-uniforms at the commands ashore, you will fail. You have to apply a hybrid model to lead both types of government personnel while simultaneously molding the separate populations into one cohesive team. It is not easy, but it is certainly achievable.

"GET COMFORTABLE BEING UNCOMFORTABLE"

Where you could confine your junior officer efforts to mastering your craft, developing rudimentary leadership skills, and execution, now much more is asked. Typically, transition into senior officer/ senior professional positions carries with it a requirement for an applicable advanced degree. For me it was a master's of science in systems management with a focus on acquisition and contracts management from the Naval Postgraduate School in Monterey, California.

A decade of junior officer experience with the addition of advanced education provides a foundation for higher level skills including critical thinking, the application of data to decision making, and an understanding of trade-off. You are no longer a "polar bear" working on the opposite poles of execution—areas where there is a clear right and wrong, compliance versus non-compliance, redlines, checklists, and so on. You will now move from the black and white world of the binary "poles" into the gray spaces. This is a messy world, so as an outstanding Marine Corps general used to say: "Get comfortable being uncomfortable."

Pictured in 2006 with two outstanding *Truman* officers at the Ney Awards ceremony for the best aircraft carrier food service operation in the fleet

INTO THE GRAY—SCIENCE OF MANAGEMENT VS. ART OF LEADERSHIP

I created and delivered a brief titled "Into the Gray" to newly promoted mid-level to senior officers and civilians many times. It shows the continuum from junior level tactical execution at "the poles" to the "gray spaces" in between. First, we need an understanding of the difference between the art of leadership and the science of management.

The science of management is the purview of junior officers and new entrants. It encompasses "know your business," simple resource management, redlines codified in policy, planning, and communication. This is an overarching focus on efficiency—getting the most from applied resources or "how the job is done."

The art of leadership is a key precept for mid-level and senior leaders. As a figurative art, it is sometimes more difficult to define. Leadership addresses matters such as vision setting and priorities, mission establishment, values, and individual redlines that are more subjective applications as determined by a leader in their present environment. There is an overarching focus on effectiveness—the end state of getting the job done—sometimes with a departure from efficiency as a controlling factor.

There is often a push-and-pull relationship between management efficiency and leadership effectiveness. An example in the abstract might be a nation at peace as compared to a nation at war. A nation at peace may tilt the scales more toward management to maximize efficiency and optimize resources for use across all elements of government. A real-world illustration would be the post-cold war peace dividend the United States politicians in the late twentieth century wanted to harvest from defense spending in favor of interests such as debt reduction and domestic priorities.[16]

During war, especially if the enemy is an existential threat, an efficiency-driven management model gives way to effectiveness in the prosecution of war and securing the future of the homeland. Spending will rise with little concern for the long-term impact of wartime debt. Effective leaders will be accommodated even if they have foibles and faults (e.g., Sherman in the Civil War[17]—Patton in World War II[18]). Procedure, policy, and sometimes even law and the mandates of the Constitution might be infringed or temporarily set aside. A common illustration is Abraham Lincoln's suspension of habeas corpus.[19] Gray-space navigation requires a multidimensional approach and at times a shifting balance between the science of management and the art of leadership.

FROM POLAR BEARS TO GRAY-SPACE INVADERS

At the tactical level, junior officers/professionals are charged with simple execution and can afford to be polar bears. Junior officers operate at the extremes of obvious situations of right vs. wrong, black vs. white, compliance vs. noncompliance, go vs. no go. It is a binary world that starts in boot camp, OCS, or corporate indoctrination, and it is often a function of rules such as law, statute, hard company policy, "shall" clauses in contracts, personnel management structure, and obvious ethical standards (e.g., lie, cheat, steal). It is a binary zone requiring little interpretation. The right answer can be determined fairly easily and quickly.

Gray space is a term denoting the mixing of the basic colors of black and white into gray. In other words, a balance of priorities and resources where one seldom has a complete win and often a partial loss. Polar bears can function and find success with a can-do attitude—the figurative "cheery aye-aye and snappy salute" followed by execution of orders. It is the simple science of the black and white world of junior officer management that gives way to the art of leadership in the senior officer gray spaces.

TRADE-OFF: GRAY-SPACE CURRENCY

Critical thinking is—well—critical. It is an environment where examination and interpretation of data should drive decisions. *Trade-off* is finding an acceptable balance of competing interests, resources, constraints, and the value of time. Critical thinking and trade-off are keys to the gray-space game of finding an acceptable yes. You live outside the comfort zone because at the close of every decision meeting there are winners and losers. Participants may be bestowed or denied resources. Simultaneously, egos are stroked and bruised, relationships bolstered and fractured as a function of the trade-offs of limited and shifting resources in pursuit of the best solution on the table. The gray-space trade-off means you are not engaged in a zero-sum game; rather, you are riding the ebb and flow of resources.

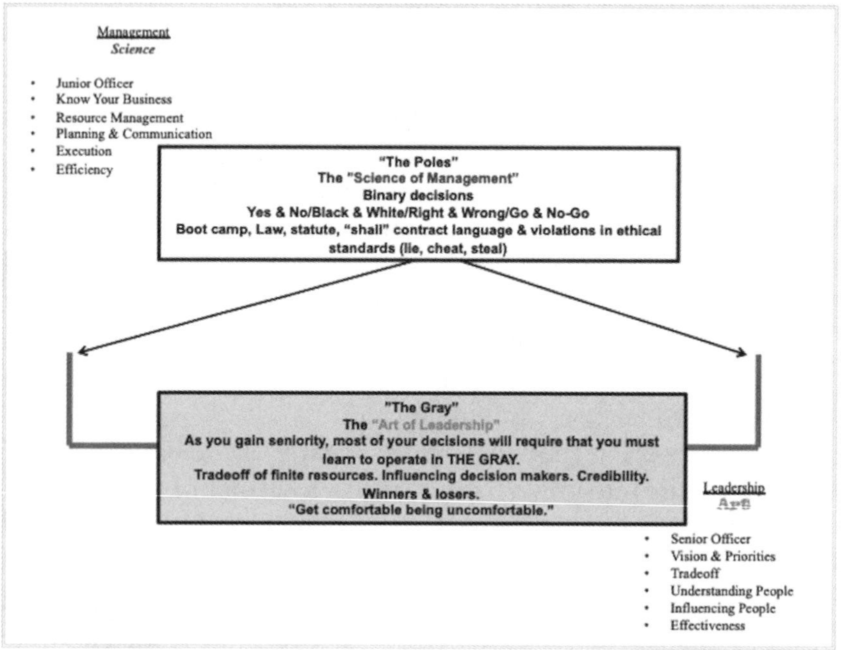

"Into the Gray" From a training session I conducted for new senior officers and senior civilians

KNOW THE ROOM—KNOW THE MOTIVATION—KNOW YOUR ROLE

As stated previously, there are winners and losers in nearly every trade-off. Relationships increase in importance as you increase in seniority, stature, and responsibility. As such, knowing the stakeholders to include the nature of important engagements is essential. Questions that demand clarity:

- Who chairs the meeting?
- What is the agenda?

- What are my equities/my team's equities/my boss' equities?
- How do the agenda items align with the greater unit/company mission?
- Who are the representatives in the room?
- Are they principals, deputies, or placeholder representatives?
- What is your role—principal speaker, deputy to the principal, or tertiary representative for your boss or team?
- Are you at the table or on the wall?
- Will you be an active participant or are you charged only with fielding background questions and recording notes?
- Who are your allies in the meeting and who is your adversary?

These are all very important for you to adequately find your fit in the decision meeting.

PREPARE YOUR NARRATIVES—HAVE DATA AT THE READY

As a mid-grade to senior officer/professional, you are now charged with critical thinking. This is more than simply ad hoc cogitation and tap dancing in meetings. The road to afterthought status is littered with the bones of young professionals who believe they can field the "hot grounders" in a meeting without preparation. As time permits, you must "murder board" important upcoming meetings with your colleagues/staff as a means of preparation. Establish all the potential narratives that may arise from the agenda and your counternarratives to support your position and refute lines of questioning (sometimes attacks from your adversaries).

Bring data to the table to support your narratives. I am sometimes stunned at how far into the decision cycle some organizations tread without supporting data. As a new entrant to mid-level machinations, you may find you are the only one with data at the table, and in most cases the presence of data vs. the absence of data is decisive. In short, you can be wrong with data and still win the day.

My best example is a meeting I had while in major command as a Navy captain. To set the framework—prior to my arrival, there were some misunderstandings between my command and a special interest office within the region. As a result, we received a questionable failing grade from the special interest representatives. I was at the crossroads between fighting the past grade or laying the groundwork for the reevaluation. We chose the latter. I did many visitations to the special interest office, and we established office space for their representative in our building. We were on our way to better relationships, but there was still skepticism in the special interest office and evaluation team members. About thirty days before the reevaluation, I was summoned to the office of the systems commander (the boss of my boss—a two-star admiral) who also invited to the meeting the Department of Navy representative for the special interest (civil servant from the senior executive service (SES) holding a three-star equivalency).

I did not want to undercut our efforts by fumbling through binders and reading from notes in front of this high-powered audience. I needed to inspire confidence in our reevaluation prospects and my mastery of the facts, so we prepared thoroughly for this meeting—to include surreptitious memory aids. I had my "trip binder" with clear plastic page holders on the outside. On the backside of the binder, we placed a sheet of paper with two dozen potential lines of questioning (in six-point font) we believed I could face in the meeting including hostile narratives. Beneath the potential questions were three short points in response structured in the Covello method (three points, nine words per point, not to exceed twenty-seven words total). The prepared communications also had some associated facts and figures about our performance and intended plans in pursuit of future special interest priorities. To the casual observer, the binder cover sheet appeared to be a POC listing when it was actually a cheat sheet.

The questioning went on for one hour. I fielded dozens of questions while seated at the far end of the conference table. During the exchange, I appeared to be pondering the questions one at a time while looking down at the table with the closed binder before me. In fact, I was finding the unnoticeable small print prep questions and planned responses placed in the outside cover of the binder. My responses came off confident, cogent, lucid, and best of all—well prepared.

I was given the go-ahead to handle the reevaluation at my level without upper echelon representatives (spies) being sent to monitor our team's preparation. We did a fine job in the reevaluation and regained good standing in the eyes of the special interest office. Had I simply appeared for the meeting and blathered on unprepared, I would not have inspired the necessary confidence in my superiors regarding our ability to handle a high-risk situation on our own.

You are now starting to see the building blocks that must be assembled to achieve professional success in a senior officer environment: energy, intellect, planning, communications, data, and the awareness of gray-space resources and stakeholders. We will continue to build as we proceed through the book.

AT TIMES YOU WILL LOSE—MAKE A LOSS LOOK LIKE A CONCESSION

In the gray spaces, if you don't prepare you will lose. If you do prepare, you still might lose. You must ask the questions—self assess:

- How did you lose?
- Why did you lose?
- Was it because of poor preparation?
- Was it a lack of purity in your motives—personal issue over business interests?
- Did you lose because you were silent when you should have spoken, or did you overplay your hand?
- Was it a no-win situation?

All the best preparation in the world will sometimes not be enough to stem a countervailing tide. However, if you lose, you must lose professionally and with grace. To borrow a line from a poem titled "How Did You Die?" by Edmund Vance Cooke:

The harder you're thrown, why the higher you bounce;
Be proud of your blackened eye!
It isn't the fact that you're licked that counts,
It's how did you fight—and why?[20]

I define a good loss as an honorable loss with a pure narrative, data, and a value proposition. An optimal loss is one in which it appears as though you conceded the space or resources in favor of your adversary in trade-off for future consideration to support one of your interests—also known as "payback" or in sports a "makeup call."

SET YOUR REDLINES; UPHOLD THE STANDARD

Institutional redlines are ordinarily set at the unit level or above. They are typically clear and posted on bulletin boards and are subjects of indoctrination and periodic refresher training. They can address pilferage, harassment, timecards, etc. Personal redlines differ from institutional ones in that you are applying your individual overlay to the operations to focus your team on issues YOU believe require extra emphasis.

You will see a call to set personal redlines at various points in the book. Why? Redlines may need to be adjusted as you become more senior and have increased responsibilities. Obviously the redlines move from micro to macro as you are more senior. Junior leaders may have simple redlines: timeliness, daily work, enhanced fitness, individual accountability for processes and places (maintenance facilities/storerooms), deportment, or performance. At the mid-range to senior level, redlines go more macro.

In my two tours onboard aircraft carriers, I was responsible for approximately $100 million in inventory and budget. Needless to say, we wanted to ensure accountability. A wise supply officer (SUPPO) once told me, "If they can tie dollars and a perceived lack of performance to your backside—you're fired." Sound advice from a sage officer. Our focus on accountability drove us to apply redlines as they related to the most impactful function—receipt processing and the subsequent storage of material.

In short, improper receipt processing is typically the root of evil to location audit and inventory problems. It sounds simple, but we routinely received hundreds of pallets—boxes or stacks of material measuring 4ft-x-4ft-x-4ft representing thousands of items and associated receipt paperwork. It would not take much in the form of inattention for receipt processing to compromise inventory accuracy in an environment where the institutional (cross-Navy) standard of accuracy (by percentage) was in the high 90s. We employed a no-excuses, todays-work-today policy for receipt processing in addition to storage of material. We did not want the sun to set on material and receipts left "in processing."

Fast-forward to major command at a Fleet Logistics Center. We had cognizance over Navy logistics in California among five other states. We instituted local redlines pertaining to three lines of effort: fuel operations, hazardous material management, and classified material processes and procedures. My belief was a fuel or hazmat spill (especially in California) or a loss of classified material (anywhere) were existential threats to the command's good standing as well as my continued service as commanding officer. As such, my orders were that no waivers or bending of procedures regarding fuel, hazmat, or classified material were to be assumed or granted without my expressed consent. The administration, operations, plant, equipment, tanks, piping, storerooms, packaging, shipping processes, training, etc., should ALL look as though they were operations run by NASA. Only the highest level of material condition, training, and proficiency were acceptable. ANY shortcomings in condition, departures from specifications, or procedural issues were to be reported to my staff and to me immediately—to be followed by speedy action for current mitigation and future preventative measures. Our catch phrase at the Fleet Logistics Center was we wanted to be alerted about any new problems by sundown, and we wanted all parties to be prepared to discuss corrective actions by sun-up. I also doubled down by visiting every fuel farm, hazmat storage area, and classified material vault in the southwest region routinely.

CAN'T GO TO THE PLAYOFFS WITHOUT THE PLAYERS—TRUST AND TALENT

As I was heading out to my final sea tour as the supply officer (SUPPO or senior logistician) on my second aircraft carrier, my two-star mentor and former boss advised me to look to my personnel in the wardroom and chief's mess because "you can't go to the playoffs without the players." His message, evaluate quickly the officers in supply department (wardroom) and the senior enlisted (chief's mess). "Big Deck" SUPPOs, on aircraft carriers, amphibious assault ships, and submarine tenders (repair ships), have some say as to the personnel assigned to their ships. Most spend a fair amount of time recruiting the highest quality junior officers and chief petty officers. I brought in an outstanding lieutenant commander who came highly recommended by a trusted agent (a senior SC officer I knew well) as assistant supply officer (ASUPPO). I also recruited two senior enlisted Sailors—a master chief and chief petty officer from a previous sea tour to join me.

I evaluated the records of aspiring shipmates carefully with my ASUPPO. For those pursuing assignment on board our ship, we appraised backgrounds and phoned references. Our motto was we're looking for "the two T's." That meant *trust* and *talent*, and the first "T" was more important than the second. By trust, we meant "a stand-up guy/gal" who will work hard (as much as twice a normal workday when underway), lead by example, apply critical thinking, and put self-interest on the shelf (reference USS *Boone*'s "Ship, Shipmate, Self" priority system).

By talent, we wanted the skills and experience to facilitate success. They didn't have to be Yoda, but they at least needed to be Skywalker. The final item of note for those youngsters seeking some of these plum positions: no one hires someone without (1) knowing them personally or (2) knowing someone (a trusted agent) who knows them. If you want to be a high draft pick, you have to have a well-known/high value professional reputation. Once you pass new entrant phase of your Naval career, your days of website surfing/point and click to a position of importance are over. Remember, it's relationships that facilitate your entry into competitive positions and keep you on the fast track toward your career aspirations. Relationships matter.

TALENT—"WE ARE IN THE BUSINESS OF FINDING TALENT, AND WE DON'T CARE WHERE WE HAVE TO GO TO GET IT"

As I became more senior in the Navy, I was increasingly involved in personnel actions to include accessions, promotions, and retirements for both civilians and military members. Diversity is a prevailing interest for the Navy, and I took the issue seriously. Nay-sayers sometimes decry diversity as a quota system. Not so in my experience in federal service. To be sure, a flat quota system would be self-defeating for an organization and demeaning to the high-performing members from underrepresented demographics. My notion on diversity was multi-layered and not simply a focus on demographics or how many types of associates we did or did not have. In my operations, our intent was to ensure that diversity and talent were a package deal in hiring and promotions.

The theory was: "We are in the business of finding talent, and we don't care where we have to go to get it." The talent pool could hail from the farm or the inner city, the coasts or flyover states, rich or poor areas, but the key was to go to enough places to find a diverse mix of talent. In my opinion, if you could hack the life, the family separation, the long hours, the moves, and adapt your skills with every new assignment, you were good enough for me. If you were smart, skilled, and resilient, you were on the team.

But there was one qualification beyond trust and talent. You had to join the team. You had to assimilate with all the other diverse players and become a service member or a civil servant adding value and harmony to the equation. As the natural elements of carbon and iron make the stronger alloy—steel—blended diversity from all demographics has given the United States a decided advantage over other nations in war and peace. But the separate elements must be blended (assimilated) over the crucible of fire to achieve the stronger alloy. With humans, as with the natural elements, the simple existence of diverse entities does not automatically result in the blended benefits without assimilation. We should remember the motto on the Great Seal of the United States: "E pluribus Unum." It means "Out of many, one."

The U.S. Armed Forces are especially good at rapid assimilation of new entrants through boot camp. For example, new soldiers are stripped of their individuality by removing personal clothing, possessions, and hair styles (buzz cut), and they are placed on an even platform with all other recruits through common uniforms, barracks, dining facilities, daily schedule, etc. This act of breaking down recruits to their bare existence permits the drill sergeants to engage in rapid team building—and this new team of warfighters is a blend of society's diversity—stronger, tougher, and more resilient than any single recruiting demographic.

There are numerous examples of our nation's diversity-driven innovations which have placed the U.S. as a world leader across many industries and endeavors. Wartime examples are especially instructive. From a macro perspective, World War II pitted the diverse U.S. and far-flung allied troops against the largely homogenous forces of Nazi Germany and Imperial Japan. The innovation of the Allied forces led to many asymmetric applications to overcome Axis power advantages existing at the start of hostilities.[21]

Looking at a specific example, the Navajo code talkers of the Pacific theater come to mind. They were U.S. Marines who brought their unique and unwritten language to the battlefield. Their encoded communications proved unbreakable to the enemy.[22] As far as assimilation, they added their linguistic diversity to the foundation of Marine Corps training to make a difference. To be clear, they were Marines first with their diverse skills brought to bear to win the day. Other examples of achievement by diverse teams with a singular focus occur every day. The talent is there. We just have to be willing to expend the energy to look for the talent to create winning teams.

PROBLEMS—POLICY, SUFFICIENCY, COMPLIANCE—"WE CAN RULE THE WAVES, BUT WE CAN'T WAIVE THE RULES!"

Problems beyond personal mistakes will invariably happen. These problems usually give leaders cause to review policy and procedures in search of a root cause. Very often, some leaders dive straight into addressing issues at the micro level (policy change, discipline of personnel, etc.) without first looking at the broader issues. As a leader, I find a three-part schema is useful to conduct initial assessments of process problems. The assessments center upon three basic questions:

1. **Existence of policy:** Does policy exist covering this situation or process? If no—stop and address policy creation. If yes, go to question number 2.
2. **Quality of policy:** If followed, is the policy sufficient to drive processes that keep us out of trouble? If no—stop and address policy adjustment. If yes, proceed to question number 3.
3. **Compliance:** Did we adhere to the policy and procedures?

Most often, questions of policy existence (1) are answered with a quick "yes." Absent new start-ups or soon-to-be-commissioned commands, there is typically ample existing policy and flow-down procedures to address most predictable processes. In my experience, quality of policy (question 2) is more often than not a "yes." Typically, existing policy will keep you covered if followed. Sometimes policy and procedures are stale and slow to keep up with change (e.g., switch from manual to automated [internet] procedures); however, there are normally serviceable policies and procedures in place.

Compliance (question 3) is the query most frequently answered with a "no." As such, compliance is often a root cause. Why? The policy and procedures are sometimes unknown to the employees, training has lagged, overconfidence has given way to shortcuts, or simple attention to detail is lacking. As a wise admiral mentor used to say: "We can rule the waves, but we cannot waive the rules." This is great advice. Referring back to policy and procedure, or "punching the pubs" as we say in the Navy, is a necessary level of effort to process control and ultimately high-quality output.

One final note: There are people who will knowingly do wrong. If you make examinations and you arrive at frequent compliance violations, you may have a climate of rogue behavior needing to be addressed. It is also important to address the personal behavior rather than simply blaming policy and whipsawing the organization with changes in pursuit of a zero-defect model. In my experience, policy has been sufficient to the task more often than not. In such cases, punish the person and not the policy. Make an example for all to see, and that will do much more to create a compliant culture. Misplaced blame on an otherwise sufficient policy only gives wrong-doers some measure of quarter when the lessons learned are being developed.

CONTINUOUS PROCESS IMPROVEMENT (CPI)—A PROCESS FOR PROCESS REVIEW

Periodic policy/process review is important to ensure there are appropriate standards, processes, and upline reporting as necessary to protect the interests of the military unit/civilian company. For personnel new to an organization, it can be daunting taking on the multitude of daily requirements. In addition, Continuous Process Improvement (CPI) is an expectation within most organizations. CPI can take many forms from a black belt system of a finite number of experts in the organization to a more total immersion scheme as with the Toyota Production System (TPS). Each individual will have to engage in training and participate, but can a newly reporting person engage immediately and effectively in CPI? Perhaps, depending on the health of the organization and the existing CPI structure. Regardless, there is a simple process to start down the path exposing associates to both current company policies and processes and rapidly revealing areas for improvement. The three phases include:

1. Process compliance
2. Process examination
3. Process improvement

Compliance is simply a function of researching policy and processes, evaluating compliance, and adjusting where compliance gaps exist. It is a precept from the "know your business" fundamentals called out in the junior officer/professional section of the book. The act of ensuring compliance not only protects the organization from risk, but it also makes the leader conversant in the policy and processes applicable to their position.

Once compliance is established, step 2 is a deeper *examination* of the processes highlighted during step 1—the compliance phase. This could include CPI tools such as the first steps of DMAIC (define, measure, analyze, improve, control), process mapping, data gathering, time and motion studies, or the employment of a trained blackbelt to assist in examination. Once examined, the best courses of action (COAs) are examined, and one COA is selected to create the third step—process *improvement*.

Data is an important element that pervades all we do, and CPI is no exception—especially in process examination and COA selection for process improvement. The beauty of CPI is it is a structured process by which ideas can be examined, tested with data, and accepted or dismissed based on the data. In a good CPI environment, no coworker can say: "I have this great idea, but no one will listen to me." And very often the best ideas come from the lower levels of the organizations in companies with vibrant CPI.

Finally, it is important to remember sustainment or continuation in CPI is the hardest part. Very often we high-five over process improvements, better quality, throughput, less carryover, etc., and we lock in the changes as a new status quo. CPI is designed for planned review of CPI successes (and failures) to determine if there is long-term benefit or perhaps more efficiencies to be gained. Sustainment is an enduring requirement for leaders with genuine interest in the concept. The truly great CPI organizations can sustain the process of continuous improvement.

SELF-PROCLAIMED "OUT-OF-THE-BOX" PRACTITIONERS—WARNING/DANGER!

A true out-of-the-box performer who also delivers hard work, critical thinking, and who has conquered the fundamentals of the business is an incredibly valuable asset. But he/she is also exceedingly rare. More often, you will encounter the self-proclaimed out-of-the-box thinker or performer. They're usually loud, gregarious, and unfortunately lazy. They are relegated to outside-the-box operations because they got their backsides whipped inside the box where normal operations take place including standards, hard work, and accountability.

A check of past commands and commanders will usually reveal this breed of enthusiastic job candidate is devoid of credibility. They are not hard to spot. They ordinarily bring an overabundance of self-promotion. They typically offer an evaluation of current processes as silly and anachronistic, and they frequently claim to have an easy, modern-day, flip-of-the-switch solution. They sometimes manifest themselves in the form of consultants or salespersons offering simple solutions to complex problems. They are often the masters of the shortcut.

Certainly, you may choose to push a high performer out of the box with a charter to find an asymmetric solution to a tough problem, but in the abstract, one should not be permitted to work out of the box unless they have first mastered "the box." Most out-of-the-boxers have nowhere else to go. More often than not, self-proclaimed out-of-the-box players offer only a dangerous departure from the well-worn path. Beware.

CHAPTER 10

COMMAND

BACKGROUND

To understand my perspective regarding command, one must first recognize the unique nature of the officer corps in which I served. As highlighted earlier, I was a Supply Corps officer specializing in logistics. Our designation as "staff corps" (along with civil engineers, physicians, chaplains, and attorneys) means we are not eligible for command at sea; rather, we are sometimes eligible and assigned positions of command ashore. Supply corps officers and their staff corps brethren spend most of their careers in staff support of ship, squadron, or submarine commanders at sea otherwise known as unrestricted line officers (URL) or simply "line officers." Some staff corps officers find it challenging making the transition from support to command when they are selected as a commanding officer (CO) ashore.

When I entered the Navy, there was little emphasis placed by the Supply Corps community to pursue command tours ashore. The Navy as a rule placed a premium on command at sea with the line officers (aviators, surface warfare officers, and submarine officers), and the value proposition of the Supply Corps was more often seen as staff officers bringing logistics to the fight—the business professionals of the fleet. We controlled resources and protected the public trust.

This changed in 2012 when the Chief of Naval Operations (four-star admiral—Navy chief of staff—member of the joint chiefs) decreed that all officers placed in command would (1) be board-selected, (2) go through the pre-command schools, and (3) undergo 360-surveys periodically once in command. This forced all Supply Corps officers through command boards, and boards are charged with picking the "best and fully qualified." The result was the Navy then had to balance the Supply Corps' best performers between the needs of high-powered staffs as well as billets for command ashore.

With the best and fully qualified officers now winning command, these command tours became essential milestones for any SC officer who aspired for flag rank (admiral). The Supply Corps is relatively new to the command pathway to senior officer promotion. Where before, one could confine their interests to serving commanding officers, they must now develop into commanding officers (COs). To do so requires long-term study of leaders and COs to form a philosophy of what to do and what not to do when the time comes to assume the mantle of command.

COMMAND: NOTHING SHARPENS ONE'S DECISION MAKING LIKE HOLDING THE FINAL DECISION

I sought actively and was entrusted with command of four units, during three tours, totaling six years and culminating in a final command leading 2,500 associates in thirty-one locations procuring nearly $6 billion in materiel per year. Six years in command does not sound like much in light of a thirty-two-year career. However, when one considers there are no command opportunities for Supply Corps officers until the rank of commander (O5), I served in command for six of my seventeen years of command eligibility which is 35 percent. This is a lot for a Supply Corps officer as most do not receive the opportunity for command at all, and if they do, it is typically only one time for two years.

Throughout the armed forces as a whole, a select number of officers will be simultaneously blessed and burdened with the responsibility of command. For civil servants and corporate

America, the military standards of command may seem unreasonably high. For non-military, a similar brand of accountability for performance and the activities of subordinates is typically confined to the C-suite positions. Otherwise, leadership in the civilian world is more analogous to senior staff positions in the military—with the exception of sole proprietorships.

Military command is an honor, a privilege, a challenge, a burden, and a thrill all wrapped up into one experience. You set the mission, vision, values, and for the first time in your career, you get to run things your way within reason. It is a high-wire act fraught with danger where the spotlight is on you—the commanding officer. Commanders/commanding officers are given significant latitude to ensure adequate performance and maintain good order and discipline through the Uniform Code of Military Justice.

Command in the military carries greater risk-to-career than nearly any other assignments one might perform in uniform. A simple finding of "loss of confidence" by an upper echelon reporting senior, and you're out—immediately and usually without debate or redress. The working lens of a commanding officer must be different than the lens of the commander's supporting staff. A CO is ultimately accountable for everything, whether he/she is a witness to events and offenses or not. Many a ship's captain has been cashiered for events occurring in the wee hours of the morning while sleeping in their cabin because ultimate accountability is all-encompassing and unforgiving. Although they have to operate in the gray spaces of trade-off, COs are held to a no-excuses binary standard where there is little room for error and seldom a receptive chain of command for mitigating circumstances.

In my Friday mentoring sessions, I counseled newly selected commanding officers to reflect back on their COs who made tough decisions, why the decisions were made, were they the correct or optimal decisions, etc. This is an exercise in conditioning themselves to think like a CO rather than an officer in staff support. Officers in staff support are focused on supporting the CO and developing (sometimes protecting) their junior subordinates. It is considered a failure if the CO has to detach for cause (DFC or fire) a senior staff member's subordinate, so supporting staff leaders are sometimes fixated on protecting, moving, or rehabilitating shaky performers.

When, as a commanding officer you hold the final decision, good order and discipline are key concerns. Nothing sharpens one's decision making, like holding that final decision. You sometimes have to pull the rip cord on a poor performer or character-challenged subordinate to (1) extricate them from your command and (2) set the example for others. The final decision can be tough with career altering—sometimes career-ending implications.

Command is reputed as being a lonely burden, and it is. But it is also exhilarating to set your vision, mission, values and lead your team. There is little dispute; an officer who successfully navigates command will find their perspective and decision making improved by magnitudes. There are exceptions, but to most military members; command is the litmus test when determining the relative value of an officer and their prospects for greater responsibility and authority.

Joined by my father (center) and Army officer brother (right) at the assumption of my first command in 2007

ASSESS YOUR COMMAND: IS A "TWEAK OF THE SAILS" OR A "RUDDER SHIFT" REQUIRED?

A quick understanding of your new command should be established through your pre-reporting pipeline which may include trips to your higher echelon commanders to whom you will report, stakeholders, and peer counterparts. You may also receive inspection reports, climate surveys, and operational performance assessments. Once on board, you will have a one-on-one turnover process with the outgoing CO that will permit you to confirm or refine your pre-reporting impressions. What you must now decide: "What is the state of your command, and what must be done?"

Will you be "tweaking the sails" or "shifting the rudder"? In the parlance of the days of sail (and present-day sailing clubs), a major decision for a boat under competition is when to tack the vessel when sailing into the wind. Typical sail boats may sail about 45 degrees off the wind's direction, and they "come about" or tack back and forth across the wind making a zig-zag motion when sailing the up-wind portion of the course. A boat's skipper wants efficiency in the number of tacks because with each one (caused by shifting the rudder and sails from one side of the boat to the other), the boat nearly stops until it can regain boat speed going the other way.

Conversely, a skipper could simply tweak the sails. Tweaking the sails consists of minor adjustments to the existing position (e.g., close hauled) by hauling in or letting out the sheets (ropes or lines used for control of the sails) or perhaps a minor rudder adjustment to optimize boat speed at that point of sail. Tweaking the sails permits the sailboat to stay in the same general direction to improve its station among other boats, keep up boat speed, and perhaps obtain a better angle for when they must execute a tack to the other side of the wind.

As mentioned, when a rudder shift is required, the boat essentially stops, and you lose as many as a half-dozen boat lengths (you might otherwise have achieved if you stayed on the old course) before you recover optimal boat speed. In summary, you have to be sure the time is right for a rudder shift because you are essentially stopping the boat's forward motion to achieve the zig-zag course. Indecisive skippers, violently tacking back and forth, can lose all boat speed and wind up "in irons" or facing the wind with their sails luffing and not making way on any productive course.

The same is true of a command, and that is why the assessment of your command's figurative course and speed is important, so you can determine if you need to execute a figurative rudder shift or simply tweak the sails. If it is a good command, well manned, well trained, well equipped, and well maintained, you may be in the mode of continuing the policies, practices, and procedures of the previous commander. You might make minor adjustments—"tweaking the sails"—a version of following the well-worn path. With the tweaking strategy, the good command you inherited will continue to proceed much the same as under the previous commander.

Conversely, if the command is in distress, untrained, undermanned, poorly maintained, or underperforming for any reason—you may require a rudder shift or a major change in personnel assignments, policy, or procedures. Certainly, these major changes will cause near-term inefficiencies, and you may perform worse for a while until the new procedures take hold—think stopping the sailboat and losing speed in one direction as you shift the rudder to pick up boat speed in another direction to ultimately put you on a better course.

Decisiveness and good decision making are important here. If a new CO comes on board to a good operation and changes things only for the sake of change, the CO is unnecessarily hamstringing their new command. Conversely, if the new CO eschews decisive action in a poorly performing command, the commander will be continuing on the suboptimal course set by the preceding leader. So, Skipper, what is your assessment? Will we be tweaking the sails or shifting the rudder?

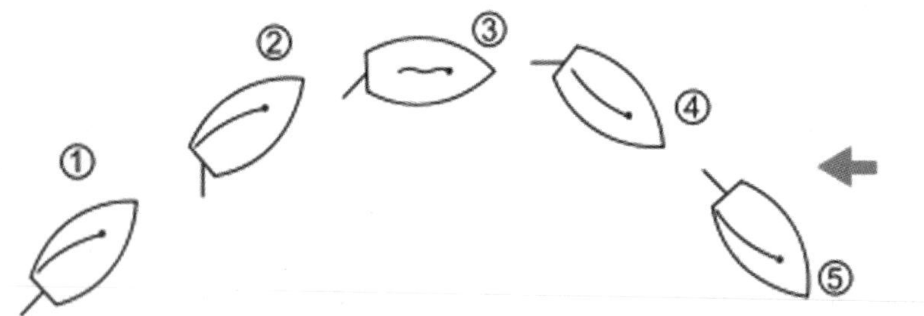

Sailboat sailing against the wind and "coming about" from a starboard tack to a port tack complete with rudder shift[23]

Exception to the rule: The sail tweak/rudder shift assessment is solid unless you are facing some type of external paradigm shift—a figurative change in the weather. If new variables are being imposed upon your command—manpower is rotated more quickly, a home port shift, an unanticipated change in leadership, increased deployment frequency, scandal in the service that causes snap-changes in standards, policy, and procedure—you may have to administer a rudder shift to an otherwise smooth-running operation.

Failure to adjust to a paradigm shift means the previously safe course is made perilous by a change in one or more significant variables. It is analogous to fog enveloping a ship underway requiring it to slow its speed, set the low visibility detail (extra watchstanders to include lookouts), and sound the ship's horn and bells every few minutes to audibly alert nearby ships of their presence. To ignore the changed surroundings and continue steaming as though you are still in clear weather may be expedient, but it is also fraught with risk.

COMMAND BANDWIDTH IS LIMITED—TUNE YOUR ANTENNA AND SET YOUR PULSE POINTS

There is only so much time an officer in command or senior leader in the civilian world can expend during a workday. The commanders/leaders need to actively assess their situation and determine which priorities are part of "the significant few" in contrast to "the insignificant many." Time, as a precious and static resource, is of extreme value to a commander. So how do you assess the best uses of your time? A former flag officer boss once mentored me, "The two most important periods for a leader are the first and final four months of a tour." His explanation: In the first four months, one is vulnerable while trying to figure out who are players, whom you can trust, what processes are safe and sound, and which ones need addressing. It is a period where you fine-tune your commander's antenna. Once you navigate the first four months, you should be able to tailor your command battle rhythm to address the significant issues demanding your time.

For first-time commanders/senior civilian leaders, it is easy to give in to a desire to handle or at least impact every aspect of your operation, but this only leads to micromanagement, underdevelopment of subordinates, and exhaustion for the CO/leader. In those first four months, you must also evaluate and develop your staff to carry out your vision and enable your team's success. You must appraise and potentially adjust mission, vision and values, publish redlines, and establish pulse points. *Pulse points* are telltale indicators that you have a problem, and further inspection is required. It is a tricky balance where a leader must be involved enough to know, but secure enough to let go.

The final four months' admonition by my flag officer mentor is also instructive. In the final four months, commanding officers must resist the temptation of "taking off the pack" and gliding into the change of command. In the final four months, there is risk for the hands-off leader when simmering problems, emerging issues, or disgruntled subordinates (looking for a parting shot) can make your departure difficult—potentially an accelerated "change of command without a band" otherwise known as a late-term firing. Bottom line: Limited command bandwidth is an asset that must be managed actively throughout an entire command tour by commanding officers and their closest staff members in support.

One of the many "great American" civil servants with whom I was blessed to serve in my first command at Defense Distribution Mapping Activity (DDMA) in Richmond, Virginia

EXERCISE CARE WHEN OPENING DOORS—CONDITION YOUR STAFF WITH "REPS AND SETS"

This is a more detailed extension of the bandwidth discussion. In pursuit of knowing and addressing everything—inspecting instead of expecting, some COs will open many doors to subjects, problems, issues, and challenges. The purpose of pulse points is to alert the CO to issues demanding their attention. Not everything requires CO bandwidth. Sometimes you have to let your staff handle things within its capability. Some problems do not require immediate attention and may resolve themselves over time. As such, sometimes a CO needs to "let the game come to them" for items that do not rise to redline violations or breaches in pulse point metrics.

An important question: What happens when, as the CO, you personally begin to engage on a subject? The answer is: you own it. You cannot unsee it. You can't close the door and pretend you do not know about it. Sometimes you can no longer delegate it, and often the expectation is, as the CO, you should address and correct the issue quickly and decisively. In other words, when you are the one to kick in the door to a problem, you sometimes forfeit the opportunity for it to be handled at a lower level that lessens your bandwidth investment and permits your staff to get the reps and sets it needs to achieve functionality.

Sometimes a quick course of action is not apparent, and letting your staff work the routine issues also allows solutions to problems mature and adapt to the situation. Bottom line—commanding officers need to focus their efforts on commanding officers' business and leave lower-level issues to the supporting staff.

EVEN WITH LIMITED COMMAND BANDWIDTH—DON'T FORGET C2—REMEMBER, NOTHING SHOWS YOU CARE LIKE SHOWING UP

Your limited bandwidth and requirement to invest your time wisely should not preclude you from the foundational requirement to get out and see your people. Why? Relationships matter—especially for a CO. It can be even more important when you are senior because unobserved subordinate commands and detachments can turn into a loose confederation of semi-independent operators—command and control (C2) goes by the wayside.

In my capacity as Pacific fleet director of logistics, fleet supply and ordnance, I placed under my cognizance two major ordnance commands with twenty-two detachments in total across eleven time zones. I was told no admiral in charge ever visited all detachments. I was committed. It took most of the full two-year tour, but we finally completed the last detachment at Diego Garcia in the final few months of my time as director. No small feat—Diego Garcia is an archipelago under the British Indian Ocean Territory about 1,100 miles south of India.

2018 and visiting Naval Munitions Command East Asia Division's Diego Garcia detachment in the far reaches of the Pacific AOR—Diego Garcia is in the British Indian Ocean Territory

In seeing the twenty-two detachments, we were able to evaluate and standardize ordnance policy, see firsthand infrastructure problems with magazines, laydown areas, roads and piers, and inform our future budget negotiations bringing rare eyewitness knowledge to the discussions. More importantly, it permitted us at Pacific fleet logistics to meet the ordnance Sailors eye-to-eye, discuss the importance of the mission, the criticality of good deportment for those stationed in foreign nations, and hear their questions and complaints. Nothing shows you care like showing up—even for those in command.

DATA-DRIVEN DECISIONS—INSIST ON DATA: "THE TRUTH IS ABSOLUTE"

We have discussed previously the necessity of individuals bringing data to the table in support of critical thinking and decision making. A CO must hold an entire staff to a standard of supporting periodic reports and methods for providing recommended courses of action with data. This is fundamental to good decision making. There is a temptation to permit a high repetition of processes to supplant the need for examination of methods and data. This is bolstered by the human nature of wanting to reduce complex problems to simple thumb rules to permit the brain to focus on other imperatives. As a result, blind spots develop in areas thought to be settled science.

A logistics example could be in arriving at the appropriate level of buffer stock to keep in storerooms to support operations. Resetting storeroom levels based on past demand is fairly common; however, forecasting and infusing future demand is often a difficult task at best—ignored at worst. An increase or decrease in anticipated operations impacts nearly all commodities including subsistence, fuel, ordnance, and parts. Good communications with stakeholders, timely and targeted validation and analysis, and adjustment of modeling to reflect the new data are all requirements to inform the decision process with the most accurate information available. To simply observe past data is to drive while looking exclusively at your rearview mirror—not a best practice.

One final note: There is a common adage, "perception is reality." This is a lazy view and damaging to the command. Perception is perception, but the truth is absolute. The CO must lead the command in pursuit of truth. Permitting a misperception to be accepted as the truth is an abdication of a leader's responsibility to operate with forthrightness and transparency. If the prevailing perception does not reflect the truth, it is unfortunate, but not irrecoverable.

Data is the tool to bring perception and truth into alignment. Data extinguishes hyperbole. Data sharpens obtuse opinions. Data curtails silly posturing and misspent emotion. Data is the cure to the "perception is reality" fallacy. Moreover, the sooner you can apply data to an erroneous perception the better, because longstanding misperceptions can be difficult to uproot. COs should endeavor to develop data and have it at the ready to inform command decision making and keep all parties honest.

VERY LITTLE THAT IS GOOD OR PERMANENT HAPPENS FAST—AGAIN, IT'S NOT THE ONE THING, IT'S THE EVERYTHING

Very often, we operate from the polar bear binary notion that we are simply one good adjustment away from a process shift and into high efficiency. For most organizations, this is a delusion and an indolent point of view. Permanent process improvement involves not only the aforementioned progression of compliance, examination, and improvement, but it also involves the longstanding requirements for policy adjustment and approval.

These adjustments include procedure modification, training, certification, performance aids, and reexamination of the processes to confirm the course of action as well as the identification of other areas for improvement. This is rarely a rapid complex transformation. In summary, command and civilian leadership positions usually hold cognizance over multifaceted interdependent processes with many variables imbedded in each process to examine and adjust.

To effect smart and enterprise-wide change, you must attack the entirety of the processes. In a complex environment—"it's not the one thing, it's the everything"—interdependent processes must be examined and refined to achieve significant improvement. It takes some time, and again, all these improvements must be codified or locked in with appropriate policy and procedural adjustments. The attempted employment of a simple one-step for permanent fix will have your organization (1) whipsawing from imbalance, (2) returning to the old unsatisfactory processes, and (3) as one fine admiral was fond to say: "accelerating to failure."

DECISIVENESS, CONSISTENCY, PERSISTENCE, AND PATIENCE

These are four attributes or traits that are foundational for a commander to excel during their tours in charge. We mentioned firm, fair, and consistent for the junior officer/professional when leading small teams. My experience is most outstanding leaders with whom I have served possessed these traits.

First, *decisive* doesn't mean fast. It means when you get to a comfortable level of data gathering and research, you employ the "80 percent and go" rule. You want neither reckless abandon nor paralysis by analysis.

Second, *consistency* is reliability—for you, your team, and your boss. Establish patterns for executive activity and standards for data upon which your team can rely. This will permit them to exercise initiative and surprise you with excellence you can easily assess and accept. You will in turn receive reports of sufficient quality and format to be able to endorse and forward quickly up the chain of command.

Third, *persistence* is simply fixing your vision upon the long game. Near-term challenges cause short-term churn and adjustments, but really good leaders can quickly turn their attention and the attention of their teams back to the long-term mission and vision.

Finally, *patience* is understanding that in larger organizations, it takes more time to drive real and beneficial change than in smaller teams. Leaders who apply small team thinking to big command challenges may over torque their staff and teams.

These four attributes when applied in concert permit the commander or leader to achieve the regal nature of command; to bring to bear quiet confidence and inspire a pervasive level of competence throughout the enterprise.

YOU ARE NOW BIG GAME—"RETIREMENT WITH HONOR IS A FULL-TIME JOB"

Once you achieve the rank of commander—a senior naval officer—you are "big game." This is even more so when one is in command. In my mentorship counseling for new senior officers (O4s—Lieutenant Commanders (Navy/USCG) and Majors (Army, USMC, USAF)), I cover the expectations of shifting from execution focus to critical thinking, operating in the gray spaces, and the greater leadership responsibilities. I also advise them they have metamorphosized and emerged from the chrysalis of the junior officer into an eight-point buck, a white rhino, a prized stag in a shadowy hunt where mid-grade to senior officers and especially commanding officers are prey.

It bears restatement: "You are big game." All you do; all you say; everywhere you go; and how you interact with people are subject to observation and sometimes recording and reporting to higher authority. Your past civilian and military peers who used to slap you on the shoulder and laugh at sea stories about deployed wild-times recalled through the haze of hangover are now shocked and appalled the Navy, Army, and others would place you in a position of leadership over them. They shift from buying a peer a beer to recording and maybe reporting their new leader with perceived character flaws to the chain of command or IG—most often anonymously.

As such, I admonish officers at every stage of promotion from first-tour field grade to flag or general officer: "Retirement with honor is a full-time job." You must consciously tend to this crop. You don't have to be a monk, but neither can you be Otter from *Animal House*. Although the written standards are unchanged, incidents involving a senior officer engaging in college frat boy or junior officer antics can be career altering.

There is a small sector of disgruntled cubicle dwellers in every organization with nothing to lose, and they would be well pleased to lend a hand in bringing down someone more senior in the organization. That someone is now you. You should know the rules and comply. You should look at yourself through the eyes of your team, and ask yourself if you like what you see. The "What would Mom say?" or *Washington Post* headline test are good internal gauges to which you can refer. Now is not the time to be the senior officer doing his best imitation as the town drunk in the hotel bar on a business trip.

As a commander (O5) assigned to a staff ashore, I was working for an admiral, and we had a couple of folks in the building who were habitually reporting late to work and turning in poor staff work. I was preparing to read them the riot act in shipboard fashion. The wise admiral pulled me aside and counseled: (1) We were not on ship where "blunt force trauma" leadership is sometimes utilized, (2) although justified, it will be noticed by the greater office community, (3) if I were to inadvertently cultivate animas among the office, I could become a target of observation for recording of every slip of the tongue and perceived insensitivity, and finally (4) if someone were to record and subsequently report a year's worth of misspoken statements, raised voices, and events in a bad light—ANYONE and EVERYONE under such scrutiny looks like a "monster" at worst, a poor leader without empathy at best.

I took the admiral's advice. We referred the matter to the professionals in HR, and they quietly did their jobs as a staff in support. They dealt in facts, documented the situation, and developed performance improvement plans. Fortunately, I didn't swat flies with a sledgehammer that day. I learned about incremental pressure and the leveraging of staff professionals. I did not make unnecessary enemies, and neither did I become one of the big-game targets in the sights of a very small minority of disgruntled teammates. Bottom line: you must do your job, and for redline violations (lie, cheat, steal), you can go coercive. For more minor violations, leverage the greater numbers within the staff with their professional expertise.

INSURANCE: MEMORANDA FOR THE RECORD AND TRIP REPORTS—WRITE IT DOWN

We just mentioned you're "big game." Documenting what happens in close proximity to when it happens is very useful when your actions, however well intentioned, are called into question. Government-funded trips (temporary duty [TDY] orders) and corporate business trips are ripe opportunities for people to allege misappropriation of funds or poor behavior. Rapidly documented trip reports showing simple itinerary, method of travel, hotel stays, meetings, etc. are good insurance against misinterpretations of your activities.

If you build the report, ensure it is sent to someone by email—either up the chain of command or an administrative assistant. This provides a time-stamped email and attachment showing what you did or did not do. If you don't do a trip report and are questioned later, you are relegated to re-creating events from memory. There will be only limited credibility in your version of the facts. Finally, trip reports can also be used to document suboptimal situations found while on travel and to track future actions required to improve deficiencies.

Memoranda for the record (MFRs) are also a good way to document what you were thinking and the actions you took when an incident has occurred. Again, you'll want to have the MFR in your possession and in another's possession (perhaps your deputy) passed through archivable electronic means.

In one of my commands, we received an anonymous assertion in a climate survey that we had an associate who was too much a "hugger" at small office birthday parties in the breakrooms. My civilian deputy and I called in this otherwise outstanding associate, and he stated he did from time to time hug coworkers as he was in charge of the largest division, and they had many impromptu birthday celebrations. We advised him there was an anonymous complaint, and we directed him to give no more hugs or touching beyond handshakes.

We documented the counseling in a MFR signed by me and the deputy, and we kept a copy in each of our offices. We did not announce publicly our actions as the original complaint was anonymous. A few months later we received another anonymous note in an electronic suggestion box asking why nothing was done to the associate who allegedly hugged too much. The deputy and I reinterviewed the associate in question, and he denied having hugged anyone since the original counseling session. We also informally interviewed a sample of his coworkers, and they corroborated the associate's claim that he had ceased unnecessary touching in the form of hugs. We reiterated the "no-hug" direction and completed another MFR in the same fashion as the first. Again, as the assertion was anonymous, we had no one to interview or provide an accounting of our actions.

The unsatisfied complainant then made a hotline call. We were visited by an investigator who stated he was there to see if he could substantiate the offenses and to determine why command (a.k.a. me) had done nothing regarding the complaints. After interviewing a sample of personnel at the command and reading the MFRs documenting our actions and reasoning, the assertions were deemed "unsubstantiated." In addition, the deputy and I actually received praise in the final written report for our method of handling the anonymous complaints. The linchpins for us as leaders were the locally generated, time-stamped, and archived MFRs that proved we took immediate and appropriate action.

Remember, write it down.

CHAPTER 11

SKIPPER'S SEA STORIES AND SENIOR OFFICER REFLECTIONS

COMMANDER ON THE FLOOR: KNOW YOUR PEOPLE. MEET YOUR PEOPLE–IN THEIR SPACES

This is a commanding officer's extension of "You get what you inspect, not what you expect—nothing shows you care like showing up." Often extolled but seldom well executed is the focus on "our people"—"our most precious resource"—"our future." This is a role that should be completed at all costs—early in a leader's tenure, and it is integral to adding value and harmony. Knowing your people is important, but it goes far beyond familiarity with a service record or employee file. I found it fruitful to go see "the troops" or Sailors in my operations where they live and work.

On ships, it is part of the highly effective "management by walking around" strategy. At my first command ashore, I employed a "commander on the floor week" soon after arrival. At this distribution depot, I took a week to meet every worker out on the floor and in the warehouses, I learned each job from one or more associates in each functional area to include pull, pack, shipping, receiving, storage, inventory, and salvage. I tried my hand at driving support equipment, using barcode scanners, scales, and industrial pulpers.

Aside from learning people and processes, I discovered quickly we had some climate problems at this particular depot—a lack of trust between supervisors and depot warehouse workers. I continued spending a part of every day on the floor meeting and getting to know the people (in addition to watching processes and learning more with every interaction). I tried to learn names, hometowns, favorite sports teams, kids, family issues, health issues, and so on. It began to work as I built some rapport and good will. Still, there were those who did not buy in to my sincerity.

One gentleman was especially skeptical of the new commander with the farm boy accent. I would see him on his forklift every day, and he was often terse. I learned over time he was a substitute preacher in his church and often delivered Sunday sermons. Furthermore, he was a source of strength to the workforce because of his ministerial experience. I began a habit early in the week asking what he or the other preachers talked about in their sermons the previous Sunday. He would tell me, and I would respond with the subject of the sermon delivered by my own parish priest in a local Episcopal church. Sometimes the conversations would shift to a short discussion or debate of sorts about faith.

As a former farm kid who was present in church several times a week—a graduate of over a decade's worth of Sunday school, I was able to joust and parry with the preacher fairly well. I began to break the ice with this man by displaying knowledge and interest in a passion of his—his occasional Sunday sermons. We found our common ground. We developed a mutual respect. Over time, I think we had a blooming friendship. He would back me up on the floor on occasion when it may not have been very popular to do so. When I departed three years later, he delivered the invocation at my outgoing change of command.

That first week as "commander on the floor," I also determined we had to change the demographic mix of our civil servant leadership. We had no minorities as senior staff or supervisors, yet the preponderance of the workers in the warehouse were from various minority demographics. We adjusted the hiring processes at the depot. We found some highly capable applicants, and we were able to hire some folks in supervisory positions who looked like the folks on the floor—further improving our climate.

The good will and loyalty established in my first weeks on the floor did much to set the tone for some noteworthy goals we achieved over the three-year command. We had some fine relationships at this tour. I returned for an impromptu visit as an admiral a decade later. Many had moved on, but some I remembered were still on the job. It was a touching reunion full of surprised expressions and as I often say, "big hugs and kisses." That was my first experience in command, it went well, and I will treasure the memory and lessons learned into my old and gray days. It all began with meeting the people "in their spaces."

"THE BIG SHIFT" AT THE RICHMOND DEPOTS

I entered my first command tour at the rank of commander (O5), and I was placed in charge of a unique distribution operation for our joint warfighters consisting of the preponderance of DoD's maps, charts, geodesy in both paper and digital media totaling sixty million items. For most of our warfighters, if you were utilizing a map to move your unit over ground, a chart to fly or navigate at sea, or geodetic material to target the enemy, it came from my operation.

The first depot was called Defense Distribution Mapping Activity (DDMA). We had the wholesale storage and transshipment operations at our headquarters in Richmond, VA with nine retail map support offices (MSOs) around the world. We were all-government workers with a civilian-heavy team at the HQ, and we were military service member dominated in our manpower at the retail MSOs. We also had one of the largest repositories of classified material in DoD with 1.4 million pieces.

There was another depot in town as well, and it stored and shipped hazardous material to DoD customers along with a minor parts mission. This other depot called Defense Distribution Depot Richmond, VA (DDRV) was one of the largest concentrations of HAZMAT in the world consisting of 4.2 million square feet of storage. Shortly after my arrival to the map depot, the civilian director of the HAZMAT depot fell ill and had to take extended time off. I was given temporary command that soon turned into a dual command for the duration of my three-year tour.

The HAZMAT depot was converting from an all-government, civil servant operation to a corporate civilian contractor activity, and there were some challenges. In addition to indoctrinating the corporate contractors to the work, we were responsible for trying to place the 100 government civil servants who were soon to be out of a job to make way for the contracted operators. The placement regulations dictated we give priority to the workers who served with the government the longest; consequently, our newly arrived, younger workers were the most at risk to be out of a job.

For the soon-to-be displaced government workers, we placed all but sixteen personnel in other government jobs with a small number choosing to retire. Meanwhile at the mapping depot, we had an aging workforce, and I received permission to offer a variable separation incentive to around twenty workers who would receive a cash payout to retire in the following ninety days. We would then hire younger workers as replacements to infuse some youth into the workforce. We combined the two HR initiatives.

The first move was to offer the incentive at the mapping depot, and I had a little trouble finding a few volunteers. It was a pretty easy option for the small collection of roughly a dozen workers who didn't like my leadership style and our drive for CPI, and they made it well known. We basically offered the incentivized exit that carried with it the added benefit of not having to work in our operation humming with change through process examination and improvement. The disgruntled few took the deal as well as a handful of really good teammates I would have gladly retained. I then offered the vacated jobs to the sixteen workers from the HAZMAT depot who were the low priority, youthful, unplaced government workers.

In two moves, we first incentivized the exit of the unhappy few from our mapping depot ranks. Simultaneously, we replaced them with young workers from the HAZMAT depot. These former HAZMAT civil servants were extremely grateful we found map depot jobs for them at the last minute so they could continue their government service. The older mapping workers, a majority of whom I won over by walking the warehouses and getting to know them, were joined by an infusion of sixteen youthful HAZMAT depot transfers who believed they owed their jobs to me.

There was very little unchallenged grumbling on the floor for the duration of my double command tour. Moreover, we retained in government service all our workers who were in danger of job loss. We found good success at both depots in Richmond. At the end of my three-year tour, I had the unique distinction of passing two command flags to two incoming commanders at a dual change of command representing both depots.

CPI—SEIZE THE OPPORTUNITY

DDMA was the mapping activity where we had a strong operation from the onset. We hosted a two-star general, two echelons up in the chain of command who took particular interest in our operation as he was looking for a depot to prototype a lean distribution model based on the Toyota Production System (TPS). At the time, we were not one of the depots under consideration, but the general was impressed. He asked if we would be interested in leading the way at DDMA, and I enthusiastically volunteered.

We were provided consultants with TPS experience as former Toyota employees. The previous depot commander was excellent, and he had unknowingly established two key foundational elements for our CPI challenge: (1) He cross-trained all employees for 120 days in two other disciplines outside their primary job descriptions and (2) He built a good, networked training center that would prove integral to the upcoming TPS-style training our entire workforce would have to complete.

We were able to leverage the previous commander's work and start immediately into the immersion training all TPS employees undergo. We established better standards, pictorial job aids, lean check-act boards, became masters at batch identification, and resource requirements (people and the material handling equipment). We completed eight major CPI efforts leaning out half the operation in the first year and completed the other elements in the second year. We started with the major processes including pulling of material, packing, shipping, and receipt processing. We followed up with inventory management, accountability, and salvage operations.

We improved quality and throughput by 59 percent and 36 percent respectively and lowered carryover by 69 percent. Our team members with the best ideas were wage-grade fork lift drivers and packers. The solutions came from the worker level to leadership for data application, evaluation, and execution. Our consultants communicated our work to their previous Toyota cohorts, and our team of blue-collar TPS experts was invited to Toyota's North American Parts Center as well as the manufacturing facility. We compared notes with the Toyota leadership and left them impressed with our transfer of TPS principles to government depot operations. It was a great effort by our team. We were decidedly more efficient and agile. But it all started with a visit to our facility where we impressed a key stakeholder followed by a discussion, an offer of an opportunity to lead the effort, and acceptance on our part.

SIMILAR "SHOW UP" LESSON IN MAJOR COMMAND—NEVER DOUBT THE POWER OF EYEWITNESS EXPERIENCE

"Major command" in the Navy is a designation for most second-time command opportunities typically bestowed upon Navy captains. In my case, major command was the Fleet Logistics Center—San Diego, and we were responsible for Navy logistics support throughout the six-state southwest region. This meant that, in addition to the fleet units, we were also responsible for logistics support to eight installations to include smaller detachments and annexes in California and Nevada. As such, we had a footprint with site directors, officers in charge, and associates serving in eighteen locations.

I was determined to visit each person (in person) at all eighteen locations in the first ninety days. I did so, including our isolated Sailors on St. Nicholas Island and San Clemente Island. This gave me instant identification with our teams in the field, the ability to convey my command philosophy, and an eyewitness view of our plant, equipment, and facilities. I was also able to meet the unit and base commanders who were our major customers. These installation commanders were also Navy captains in major command. These were important relationships that would pay big dividends when we engaged jointly in problem solving throughout the region, and the rapid forming of these relationships was a by-product of the "show up" strategy.

As FLC San Diego commander, I was also responsible for fuel operations on these bases with millions of gallons of petroleum stored in tanks—sometimes in populated areas. I had little knowledge of fuel management although the Supply Corps has a small contingent of officers who specialize in the discipline. To "catch up" on my knowledge, I took some voluntary online DoD fuel management courses. During my ninety-day tour of our detachments in the region, I also made sure to spend ample time with the fuel teams, walking the transfer lines, climbing every petroleum tank, and asking detailed questions of the operators in the control stations. The messages were clear: (1) I care about fuel management; (2) I am no expert, but I am willing to learn; (3) I will hold you accountable; and (4) I'll be back every 120–180 days to check on the operation.

By the time I finished the ninety days, I had a solid working knowledge of regional fuel operations, who served as experts, and most importantly the tanks, lines, and pumps requiring maintenance. My reporting senior, a one-star admiral remarked that I had a better sight picture of the region, the customers, and our plant and equipment after only ninety days than many of our counterpart commanders.

I engendered immediate credibility with this hard-charging admiral who placed a premium on commanders taking command. Owing to my quick grasp of the regional picture, my one-star boss showed the professional courage to let me run the show with minimal interference in the southwest region—freeing him to spend his valuable time on emergent issues in other regions.

There were added benefits to the ninety-day show-up strategy. In future discussions with repair facilities, resource sponsors, and my admiral bosses, I had firsthand, eyewitness knowledge of the situation. When trade-off debates occurred about resources, I had leverage over others at the table who had not actually seen the condition of the facilities, and that can be powerful—sometimes decisive leverage. In deliberations regarding application of resources, those of us who cared enough to "put eyes on the situation"—who "spoke with the operators on the ground" possessed a compelling case. It may not have always been a winning case, but it was not easily dismissed. I frequently utilized my eyewitness accounts to our advantage when battling for resources. This is another key manifestation of "you get what you inspect—not what you expect—nothing shows you care like showing up." As a leader and advocate for your command, eyewitness knowledge permits you to convince the serious stakeholder and easily dispatch the unstudied challenger.

Major command—inspecting damaged fuel lines at Naval Air Facility in El Centro, CA

COMMUNICATE YOUR WAY OUT OF A PROBLEM—FLEET LOGISTICS CENTER (FLC) SAN DIEGO

I was board-selected for major command (typically a command tour for a Navy captain O6) in 2014. I received orders to report to FLC San Diego in the summer of 2015 relieving one of my oldest and closest compatriots in the Supply Corps who left me a fine operation. As mentioned previously, we were responsible for Navy logistics to all installations and operations in the six-state southwest region.

There was only one area my predecessor was working but had not reached a conclusion, and it involved the small business efforts in our contracting shop. Several COs earlier, there was a communication mix-up regarding the date of a site visit resulting in a perceived slight to the southern California small business regional office. Personality conflicts arose on both sides. Subsequently, a poor assessment was issued regarding our compliance with laws and regulations requiring the use of small businesses to provide products and services to the fleet whenever possible. Although my predecessor expertly answered the inquiries of the small business office, and his contracting team exceeded targets for small business awards, his appeal to reverse a poor grade on a years-old inspection (from before his command tour) were rejected.

Then our only avenue was to score well on a reinspection that would modify the previous assessment and keep us in good standing with the regional small business office as well as the Navy and DoD small business leadership. I planned a trip to a detachment near the regional office in Los Angeles. While on the trip, I decided to detour and make a quick stop to try and leverage the adage "Communications: the root of all evil when you don't have enough, and it cures all ills when you apply more."

The SB office accepted my request. The twenty-minute appointment went on for several hours where we had a healthy back-and-forth regarding "how we got here" and "how we could move to successful passing of the reinspection." I knew three things: (1) All interested parties from Washington, DC to California thought our contracting and execution were outstanding—even award-winning except this one particular office (2) Goodwill among other small business entities was immaterial as this one office was going to be conducting the reinspection (3) The penalty for failing the reinspection could have impacted our authority to award contracts which would have been fatal for the San Diego FLC as contracting was one of our primary lines of effort.

To start, I protected my team and the position of our preceding commanding officers as I politely pushed back on the assertion we were a failing operation. I conceded there were things that could have been done differently, and we could improve. I made friends with the office members who were friendly and at least put a face to a name with those who were not. The "show up" adage was applicable in this situation. The small business officers now knew me, and they knew I was serious and approachable. I was also a contracts expert having held an unlimited federal contracting warrant three times in my past. I was no longer a faceless person with a CO's title.

One major development was I agreed to provide office space to their San Diego small business representative, so we could more quickly reach solutions and build rapport. We welcomed the representative to our building, treated him as part of the FLC crew, and quickly developed team spirit and a productive relationship. Whenever the inspectors from out of town made the trip, their representative on the ground was in all likelihood going to give us passing—perhaps glowing remarks about our methods of doing business.

We also hedged our bets by traveling to meet people within my own chain of command and the Washington, DC small business chain of command at the one-star, two-star, and three-star level. I communicated with everyone involved and EVERYONE knew, EVERYONE provided input, and EVERYONE approved of our recovery plan. By extension, they were now implicitly on our team.

By happenstance, one of the leaders in DoD's small business hierarchy (I met and briefed during my travels) was tasked to attend the reinspection as an observer. As he was already aware of our plan, he was ready to comment in an informed manner as the reports came in on the reinspection. We drew two inspectors from the small business office. One was sympathetic to our narrative and recovery plan, and I perceived the other was less so. Regardless, we got a good, tough assessment, and we passed. We were back in good standing and had a more solid if still shaky relationship with the Southern California small business office. In the end, poor communication and misinterpretation got us into the predicament, and good communication got us out.

"BRINGING IT HOME"—FAMILY APPLICATION OF FARM AND NAVY LESSONS

"Prisoner of Dad"

Having a family is one of God's greatest gifts, but family operations take work to keep things in balance. Competing careers were a challenge, especially as mine required moves every couple of years and my wife's career required her to follow. We established this "lead and follower" relationship between our careers that worked well—but not without effort. Brooks bore the brunt of the burden of flexibility to accommodate my career. Still, she was highly successful as a registered nurse—mostly in emergency departments, and she was licensed in seven states.

Our children and their interests were also a tough task. The constant moves and changing environments required us to try to make the inner workings of our home life as consistent as possible—no matter where we lived. Borrowing from my parents, we emphasized the importance of school and church, but there was no farm to ground the kids. We chose sports, and both kids excelled at various activities at different times in their lives. They ultimately left sports behind to grasp opportunities at higher education, careers, their own families, and beyond.

In their formative years, we had to have consistency in the house. I often joked that my policy with children was like our national policy with terrorists—you don't negotiate. This was not completely true because negotiation became necessary as they got older and had trade-off choices between competing productive courses of action. Still as small children, I was a fan of establishing clear standards or redlines and implementing reactions for actions that crossed the barriers. A few anecdotes stand out.

As one boss once told me: "Kids don't get easier as they age, they just get different." This is certainly true. The redlines changed as the kids aged, but they were there. On my final two ships, my family was located in Richmond, Virginia—ninety miles away from my ship's homeport of Norfolk. I would come home on the weekends when we were not at sea. Our children hated the periodic weekends when my wife drew a twelve-hour hospital shift on Saturday or Sunday as their fortunes were left in my hands.

Brooks typically left them a list of work to do, and in teenage fashion, the kids usually executed a half-hearted effort just before one of us would get home. For me, I replicated a ship's "plan of the day" or POD for our weekend activities. I would list out our work, play, meals, homework, kids' chores, etc. in thirty-minute increments from dawn to dusk. I would post it on the refrigerator, and we would check off the work completed as the day passed. My kids hated the POD calling it "prisoner of Dad," and the wailing and gnashing of teeth could be heard across the neighborhood. Still, it was instructive to the kids on how to organize team efforts, and we plowed through a lot of required activities when we operated under the POD system.

Cat-tales

To walk by a suboptimal situation or ignore a failure to follow orders constitutes tacit approval and encourages further bad behavior. Such Navy lessons sometimes work well at home.

My daughter had just been presented with a car for her sixteenth birthday. It was a used Ford Focus, and she was justifiably proud to have a car. One morning that summer, I was preparing for work, and she was preparing for a day out with friends. I noticed the cat's litter box (a cat she picked out some years earlier) was full. I called to Elizabeth and asked her to clean out the box before she departed. She replied, "Yeah, Dad."

After several reminders, I was nearly ready for work and no effort had been applied to the litter box. So I took the opportunity to scoop and bag the cat poop to help matters along. I shouted to Elizabeth and said I had bagged the litter and left it by the door for her to take to the trash. She replied, "Yeah, Dad." I went back to the kitchen to grab the keys and briefcase; meanwhile, she darted out the door to meet her friends out front who were picking her up for the day's activities. I looked down, and to no surprise saw the plastic bag full of cat contents.

On my way to the trash can I passed my daughter's car, and the practical joker in me, generations in the making, took over. I thought, *Maybe we need an "attention-getter" here*. I opened her car, wrapped the loops of the bagged cat poop around her turn signal lever, and closed the door. Off I went to work as the sun rose for a smoldering 90-degree summer day. She arrived home later to find her car stinking of day-old, hot-baked cat poop.

In the mid-afternoon, Brooks called me from her ER station at the hospital. She said, "Our daughter called, and she is very upset. What did you do to Elizabeth's car?" I said, "Oh nothing—the car is fine." She pressed the issue, and I told her the story. My wife said, "You deal with her—I don't have time" and ended the call. When I got home, my daughter and I had a long talk about taking responsibility for her cat, following directions, and so on. She never forgave me for stinking up her car, but she also was much more diligent about taking care of the cat and following Dad's attention-getter. Funny, my daughter is now a wife and mother of two, and they don't have a cat.

Snow day

Self-awareness and motivation are important lessons to teach youngsters. My son was not immune to farmer and sailor training sessions on my part. During my first command, I was returning from visiting one of our detachments in Waegwan, South Korea. It was a sixteen-hour flight, and I landed at dawn in Richmond with the streets blanketed from a recent snowstorm. I drove my car slowly from the airport navigating the not-yet-plowed streets. I made it to our house and knew I would never make it up our steep driveway, so I parked on the street. I was certain the snow plows would soon be making their rounds, and they would cover my car in snow—or potentially hit the car, so I had to get it up the driveway's incline. I figured it would take me about ninety minutes of hard shoveling to clear the pavement. After sixteen hours of flying, I was in no mood.

My wife was working that day, so I expected a quiet house when I walked in. I found my son—anticipating the snow day home from school having a sleepover for a half dozen of his teenaged friends. So, after a long flight, I entered my living room to a bunch of boys in boxer shorts playing video games, snacking on the furniture, and making a mess. At this point, I channeled my farm-owning father and mother. I dropped my bags, put on my boots, and immediately deputized the boys to assist me in clearing our driveway. I rousted the youngsters and escorted them to the gear locker—our garage. I issued our one snow shovel, dirt shovels, stray pieces of plywood, and anything else to put in each boy's hands to assist in moving snow. They grumbled, and one boy asked if I would be paying them for their services. I asked if he had eaten breakfast that morning. He said "yes" and I replied "payment rendered in advance—now get back to work."

It took us about thirty minutes to clear the driveway. My son was a little embarrassed that his friends got pressed into service as human snow plows. Later that day, his friends left, and we had a discussion about self-awareness, the fact his mother and I needed to park in the driveway, being a self-starter, and advancing the family cause. He understood the lessons, and we laugh about it these days as adults.

As stated in the dedication, I was not nearly as well practiced in balancing home life and work life as I recommend in this book. I fell short many times, but life is a "gray-space" endeavor where trade-offs are necessary to advance various interests. In the end, my wife and I have no complaints and few regrets in how we managed two kids, two careers, a half dozen dogs, and one cat over so many moves.

We kept the best practices of focusing on a few consistent themes: faith, the kids' school, and their sports. We were perpetually preparing to tackle the biannual challenge of saying goodbye to our current town, home, church, schools, and workplaces, and preparing for a new duty station that would only be revealed to us a couple of months before our departure date. In balance, it all worked out. Our kids are college graduates, professionals, spouses, parents, and examples of good citizens making their own way in America. We are blessed.

Our daughter (far right) celebrating her graduation from James Madison University with her roommates in 2012

Our son, a 2014 graduate of The Citadel—pictured with me for a "ring shot" in front of the school's larger-than-life representation of the "band of gold"

CHAPTER 12

FLAG/GENERAL OFFICER—THE MILITARY "C SUITE"

ENTRÉE TO FLAG/GENERAL OFFICER AND SENIOR EXECUTIVE SUITE IS SOMETIMES ON THE MARGINS

Accession to the most senior levels of leadership is the goal of many highly driven officers and civilian leaders. The path is not always clear. For every officer who achieves flag (admiral) or general officer promotion, there are at least a half dozen others who are qualified and could do a fine job. In other words, all serious contenders for flag officer, general officer, and senior executive positions are masters of their respective trades. So, what is the deciding or decisive factor? How is the cut made?

First, relationships and visibility matter. Aspirants for pinnacle positions must be known to the masses as a top-shelf performer. Still there are many with the skills, level of expertise, and professional reputation sufficient to be selected. Often, the difference is a skill, proficiency, or experience residing on the margins. What areas, in addition to common functions add to the portfolio of an aspiring admiral, general, or chief executive? Examples could be public speaking—perhaps enhanced analytical proficiency or writing skills. Could it be you've executed HR functions as a detailer or assignment officer that gives you keen insight on the manpower you will lead? Do you have recent deployments "down range" to give you frontline insight your competitors lack? Did you accrue asymmetric skills while serving in joint duty? In short, all serious candidates can do the job—the meat and potatoes functions; however, tertiary skills may be what pushes a candidate over the top.

I spent several tours as a commander (O5) totaling seven straight years outside the umbrella of the Supply Corps. I slipped into the background and lacked visibility. Subsequently, I was offered and accepted the position of Director of Supply Corps Personnel responsible for (1) determining the future positions for all 2,300 Supply Corps officers, (2) issuing permanent change of station (PCS) orders to move the officers and (3) delivering the Supply Corps career "road show" to fleet concentration centers around the world.

In conjunction with travel to support the road shows, these responsibilities gave me access to every Supply Corps admiral in the Navy. Also, the head detailer position gave me unparalleled experience in the little known but very important field of military manpower management. The road show also gave me the opportunity to display my public speaking skills as I addressed audiences from a few dozen to several hundred for as many as three hours per interactive session.

Finally, my formative experience as the son of a school teacher meant my writing skills were strong. Good writing is a lost art, and I was deputized frequently to handle important projects demanding high quality written products. Combined with a firm foundation in the "meat and potatoes" areas of logistics, supply chain management, contracts management, service at sea, and multiple successful command tours—my speaking ability, writing proficiency, and intimate knowledge of the military HR processes were the on-the-margin skills I brought to the table when I was selected for rear admiral.

CAN THE TRAIN CONDUCTOR RUN THE RAILROAD?

You serve as a pinnacle executive: an admiral, a general, a senior executive, a chief, or chairperson. You are likely in charge of thousands of people and millions—often billions of dollars in plant, equipment, sales, revenue, etc. Your life is forever changed. Some of your longstanding friends will celebrate your success while others drift away for an array of reasons you would rather not contemplate.

The ability for others to pick up the phone and engage in one-on-one communications with you carries gravitas for your new colleagues and former peers. You have proven you can lead with aplomb at major command, directorship, or corporate subsidiary. You can drive the train. But can you run the railroad? They're related but they're not the same, and that transition will be the key to your success—or failure.

RELATIONSHIPS MATTER—COMMUNICATE TO SET YOUR SUCCESS BEFORE YOU ARRIVE

As a newly minted flag officer, it became apparent to me there would be little or no latitude for time spent getting up to speed at new duty stations. Admirals were expected to have all the answers from day one. Consequently, I wanted to be as prepared as possible as I entered my first flag assignment in Hawaii as U.S. Pacific Fleet's Director of Logistics, Fleet Supply and Ordnance. I began a process of pre-reporting communications allowing me to start work at a sprinter's pace immediately upon arrival.

First, I solicited from the admiral I was replacing (and the staff) the major stakeholders with whom we would need a good and robust relationship (customers, chain of command players, resource holders, process players, etc.). Then I created a battery of questions and made my calls. I recorded and compared all answers and had a pretty fair impression of where we were strong and weak and what overarching challenges or themes were prevalent. I also took short courses over a 10-day period at the Naval Postgraduate School for all subjects addressing Asian and Pacific history, politics, and current state of affairs.

Finally, I read several books recounting the past actions of the U.S. Navy in the Pacific area of responsibility to include logistics support during past wars.

This proved especially valuable when I was reporting to my new boss—a four-star fleet commander covering eleven time zones. In my in-brief, I dispensed quickly with the idle chitchat about the move, where we'll be living, and when can we expect our household goods shipment. I was able to articulate to the boss the major players with whom I already established a relationship and the four top challenges frequently articulated by these stakeholders. I placed the challenges in historical and political context from my course work and independent reading.

Fortunately, these key issues aligned precisely with my new commanding admiral's assessment, and I was off to a great start in the eyes of my boss. Moreover, I was able to meet with my team and display immediate knowledge of the tasks at hand. The result—instant credibility with my boss and my team as well as a strong initial foundation for relationships with all our stakeholders.

When I started to travel to see subordinates and major cohorts, we had already conducted the business related, preparatory phone conversations, so we addressed immediately the issues of the day.

A final note: put in the work—the communications reps and sets to know key players and to be known as a key player of equal station and equal standing. Set your success and get a jump on relationship building with pre-reporting communications.

SET THE TONE—ESTABLISH RULES OF ACCESS, ENGAGEMENT, AND TIME INVESTMENT

Immediately upon assuming your new position, you have to set the tone, expectations, any adjustments to mission/vision/values, as well as modification or establishment of redlines. Equally important is how your staff will interact with you and vice versa and how you will both administer the most precious of your resources—time. In your new capacity, the importance of relationships has increased even more, and your bandwidth for receiving and processing information and issuing direction is reduced.

Notice we have termed the issue as *time investment* and not management. Senior executive time is so valuable the use of it is more an investment of a precious and limited rare element than a simple resource to be managed on par with other assets. This is an especially important distinction on the high-powered staff at the three- and four-star level. I often compare a four-star burden of situational awareness as analogous to a person standing on a train platform as a bullet train passes. The admiral on the platform strains to see the blurred images in the passing train windows to try and quickly glean what is going on and determine what to do.

Senior flag and general officers—senior executive counterparts have very little time for deep dives. It is the job of the staff to bring the senior officer up to speed, sometimes with just a few phrases. It is the job of the senior officer to set the environment for success regarding the use of time. Time, access, and engagement are all-important. I observed a newly arrived, four-star admiral order the use of 20 percent "vector checks" for complex projects. He wanted brief but periodic "touch and go" meetings to quickly receive information and give direction, so his direct reports would not waste valuable senior staff manhours on a deliverable which would otherwise be rejected out of hand for missing the mark.

Who has access to the man/woman in charge, and who does not? Open-door policies are unwieldly at this level. How do you pulse the work force—what is the frequency of town halls? What is the battle rhythm of staff meetings and project meetings to keep leadership apprised of various situations and permit back and forth communications? What is your rollout plan to meet out-of-town subordinate entities and detachments? These things must be determined and promulgated immediately upon taking command or assuming a high-level leadership position. It must be a system upon which both the leader and supporting staff can rely for consistent communications.

Pearl Harbor—escorting distinguished visitors to the Arizona memorial

THE BIG PICTURE—VISION SETTING AND STRATEGIC PLANNING

In the strategic world of pinnacle leadership, you are no longer thinking within the bounds of a single tour length. A good flag officer/general officer (FO/GO) or executive player knows the type of planning for which they are responsible spans a decade in the future. In the grand scheme, you're still trying to add value, but there is more in play and much more at stake. A new senior executive first must evaluate the vision setting, planning, and achievements of his/her predecessors and determine if it is prudent to continue along the paths set forth by others.

This is a supercharged version of the "rudder shift and sail tweak" model discussed earlier. In some cases, the environmental shifts in politics, resources, unit performance, and good/bad fortune may dictate a course correction. However, if the previous plans and military/business environments are stable, the new leader may be able to align their vision with the past progress of former leadership.

There is a lot on the line for these government and corporate leaders because in both cases we are talking about vision setting and strategic planning for multi-billion-dollar organizations. Some level of adaptability must be infused into the plans, but you have only limited time to effect change at this level. Externally, the favor of the senior chain of command and Congress or corporate governing boards/investors must be engendered to continue the flow of resources. Time is of the essence to inspire confidence in your strategy and show progress. The first order of business is to align efforts within your organization.

ACHIEVEMENT OF "ALIGNMENT OF EFFORT"

As a FO/GO in command or an executive performer, the scope of your organization can be broad, and alignment of effort should cross all subordinate commanders and major staff directorates. What started with validation or adjustments to mission, vision, and values must now inform end states and strategic plans to get there. The hard task is driving your vision and strategy across all echelons.

Alignment of effort can be achieved through the creation of tiered strategic and subordinate plans. Your strategic plan should be supported by subordinate plans to enable the achievement of the end state goals. In the spirit of you get what you inspect, not what you expect, the supporting plans and status of execution must be checked—by you and not simply a functionary.

As previously stated, nothing shows you care like showing up. As such, your review of supporting plans may be a good opportunity to visit the subordinate commanders and directors to take their report on plans and execution. This is more than an enforcement tactic. Remember, you only have so much bandwidth to devote to the cause of your organization, so these complex combinations of "visit and check" make effective opportunities for FO/GO and senior executive leaders to apply a personal touch throughout the staff and down echelon.

INFLUENCE THROUGH EXTERNAL COMMUNICATIONS—RELATIONSHIPS ARE OF PREMIUM IMPORTANCE

The biggest fallacy of the twenty-first century says relationships no longer matter. To some in leadership, business can be transacted and success can be achieved with nameless and faceless electronic interactions. Some aspiring leaders permit their interpersonal skills, standards of personal appearance, and preparations for the "thirty-second speech" to atrophy thinking such abilities are anachronistic. Nothing could be further from the truth. In fact, it is the more rare, present-day interpersonal interaction that makes live communications and relationship development a greater imperative than in the past. For admirals, generals, and senior executives possessing limited time to invest, this is doubly so. There are no throwaway encounters.

I am lucky in this regard. I am my father's son, an extrovert, and I have no fear meeting new people. I am actually energized by it. This has served me well in executive positions. Leveraging the adage, "Communications: The root of all evil when you don't have enough—cures all ills when you apply more" is key. This adage is supercharged, steroid-infused, and accelerated to the redline as you reach pinnacle positions.

External communications are even more weighty because you have to influence resource managers, peers, stakeholders, and customers. You have to set a narrative as to the value your team adds and what you are doing to continue or improve your efforts. You can never start too early in this endeavor. “Commanding down” should be old hat by now. “Influencing up” is now the critical task. Relationships, communications, trust, and credibility are key to being able to move the needle with higher echelon commanders and resource stakeholders.

CREDIBILITY IS THE CURRENCY OF THE REALM

In the macro, rough, order of magnitude world of admirals, generals, and senior executives, there is an enhanced trading commodity. Now, the manner of organization, strategic plan, smart communications, critical relationships, planning and preparation, and presence of capable talent create a most critical alloy—credibility. Credibility is an intangible, yet it is very important. It is analogous to black holes in space—you know they exist only by the presence of other indicators (e.g., the bending of light, gravitational anomalies).

There is no metric or gauge for credibility. The best indicator I have seen is the time your peers and superiors will devote to you and your communications. Are your phone calls answered and returned quickly? Do you have generous latitude when you speak in public and at governing meetings? Are your emails followed by quick responses indicating acknowledgement of your message followed by assurances of collaboration? Are you a frequent winner with resource trade-offs? If so, you’re on solid ground.

Conversely, if you require several calls to get access to a stakeholder; if you’re often cut off in meetings; if someone feels the need to translate your narrative; if you get the short end of the resource allocations; you may have a deficit or suboptimal credibility. This is key because credibility is required to influence and accrue resources to achieve milestones, strategic goals, and blaze the trail toward your vision.

CHANGE MANAGEMENT—"IT IS PRESSURE OVER TIME THAT MAKES THE DIAMOND"

As a Navy captain, I coined this analogy to remind the team and me that as we increase in seniority and responsibility, quick wins and snap decisions are more and more rare. Rather, the driving of real change at senior levels is a function of coordinated efforts across an array of functions to include planning, financial resources, policy and procedure, stakeholder management, bolstering alliances, addressing detractors, data management, and analysis to name a few. Remember our lesson from the Navy captain charged with fixing a hard-luck ship: "It's not the one thing, it's the everything."

Official photo commanding Defense Logistics Agency Land and Maritime

All this takes time to bake in desired organizational change, and it can be frustrating. Nevertheless, planning is of premium importance, and alignment of effort among your staff is equally so. Some leaders seek change by sending their subordinate commanders and directors out to cultivate their own areas of excellence in the hopes someone will discover the next big thing. It has the perceived added benefit of infusing competition. This "dog fight" strategy carries risk because resources may be squandered and alignment of effort could be shattered. Persistent and coordinated focus on the long-game is key. Vision setting, long-term planning, and synchronized execution apply the pressure over time creating the diamond-level performance.

HAVE AN AGENDA—DESIGNATE A MANAGING PARTNER

As FO/GO or C-suite leader, your time is valuable, but so is the time resource of your subordinate commanders and staff directors. There is nothing more frustrating than a wanton waste of executive bandwidth. Examples include conducting meetings with no agenda, too large an agenda, idle chitchat, staff sausage-grinding about other matters interjected into the discussion, and gratuitous application of the mute button to overtly discuss things the greater audience is not welcome to hear. You and your team deserve better, so make it better.

I find a good course of action is the designation of a managing partner to support you in the spirit of a partners' meeting at a law firm. All partners have a say, the senior partner has sway, but the managing partner runs the meeting. This is a great tool to set the tone of professionalism and seriousness in the meeting.

As a Navy captain, I was the operations officer for a Navy logistics command headed by a two-star admiral. We periodically had meetings across the enterprise with senior staff leadership in the room and ten subordinate or supporting commanders on VTC. I prepared for the meeting by drafting issues for consideration, confirming consensus, and gaining approval of the agenda by the commanding admiral.

During the meeting I opened the event, with a short and terse welcome to the meeting and announced the chairman (admiral). I then alluded to the agenda but didn't take time to read every item (most Naval officers and staff members can read). I offered the chair opening remarks. I then offered a general call for opening comments. Note, I did not go down the roll call and ask individually for opening comments. This is for two reasons, (1) it is a time waster and (2) you lose control of the meeting early. I then would call forth the first briefer and introduce him/her (e.g., Captain Smith), and the first item would be briefed. Upon close of the first item, I would do a general call for question/comment. Again, no roll call of all stakeholders because all senior officers may feel compelled to opine and outdo other meeting attendees.

Finally, I would ask the chairperson (commanding admiral) for questions/comments. If there was a decision—I would see if the boss wanted to do a unilateral table slap (approval) or if a vote was necessary. I would hold a vote by individually calling the roll and on to the next briefer and so on. The meeting would be executed and concluded with meeting minutes to be forwarded to all concerned within two workdays.

Enablers to effective meetings are read ahead versions of the draft briefs (passed to attendees no later than twenty-four hours before the meeting) and having briefers who employ "bottom line" briefing. No reading of a dozen bullets per slide is permitted. Also, slide counts for briefs should be realistic. A good rule of thumb was no greater than eight slides per half hour for a flag-level brief. Do not accept sixty-slide PowerPoint presentations for a twenty-minute briefing period.

Remember: It does NO GOOD to have discovery learning of the briefs at the meeting by the chair and attendees because we could not assemble the information before the meeting commenced.

Recommendation: Strike late providers of information from the agenda to infuse discipline in the process. Bottom line: The meetings must be dependable events upon which you and your team can rely to pass communication, make decisions, and set future agendas in an efficient and effective manner. These are not water cooler gossip sessions in disguise.

LEARN TO READ PEOPLE—THEN KEEP IT TO YOURSELF

Learning to read people is innate for some and learned behavior for others. For the naturals, there is little more to say. For those willing to learn, reading people lends itself toward one's ability to read the room. The first step is knowing people, their professional titles, and their backgrounds. Assessing body language, changes in voice tone, and the array of nonverbal signals confirming or betraying the words coming out of another's mouth are key to reading a person or room full of people.

As a leader, you can judge the veracity of one's statements, enthusiasm, and forthrightness through positive body language cues. Examples include nodding, leaning forward, note-taking, etc. You can detect an underlying lack of respect, impatience, and potential disloyalty through negative indicators such as feigned boredom, finger drumming, phone checks, crossed arms, and spontaneous sidebar conversations. Once you string together a trend of behavior, you can categorize people as trusted agents or less than trustworthy or somewhere in between. You may temper your actions privately based on what you read. Subordinate assignments requiring a special level of trust should be assigned accordingly. Otherwise, you can assign personnel more indifferently to common tasks. These private personnel assessments should be kept to yourself.

The primary reason to keep these impressions to yourself is if a half-hearted subordinate or counterpart is aware of your notion, they may stop the pretense of loyalty and enthusiasm. You may then have an overt poor performer on your hands. And you must remember, you cannot purge someone from your operation for just being a half-hearted follower. So either way, you'll have to deal with all the members of your team (good and bad) for the long term. The secondary reason you should keep it to yourself is you could be wrong. To summarize: leaders are well served to observe, assess over time, and keep the assessments under wraps unless a redline is crossed.

CULTURE EATS STRATEGY FOR BREAKFAST—BUT DON'T FORGET THE STRATEGY

This quote is from Peter Drucker, and most agree culture is extremely important to the long-term prospects of an organization. I would also say a well-constructed strategy is also an existential requirement, so I look at culture and strategy as more equal players where the absence of one means failure for an organization. Still, a positive culture is sometimes difficult to achieve.

I commanded one organization where the outstanding leaders before my arrival created a "constellation of councils"—sixteen entities to be exact. These councils, special emphasis programs, and professional organizations covered among other things supervisors, directorate leaders, training, the various demographic subgroups, and wellness. The presence of this constellation gave multiple avenues for associates to voice ideas, concerns, and potential solutions.

A key enabler to councils seeking to propose change was the continuous process improvement program. As mentioned, the beauty of CPI is it provides a structured mechanism to bring ideas forward with associated data to support (or refute) the notions. The ability to advance ideas in a structured and data-driven environment permits all associates to play a part in influencing the trajectory of the command. CPI was infused throughout this model. The constellation of councils represented an immensely powerful collection of tools, and the climate surveys for this organization were very strong.

I added to the command a family atmosphere approach. I asked the command to look at every associate as family and every day at work as a family reunion. If you imagine a family reunion, they're all similar. There is gathering of people and a table with the oldest member of the family (let's call him Uncle Lou) present for what might be his last reunion. How do the family members (friendly or not) act around Uncle Lou? They protect each other's feelings. They leave the foul language and snarky social media tactics at home. They approach each other with mutual respect. This was the picture I wanted every associate to envision when they came to work. When you look at each other as "family" (brothers and sisters), it is more difficult to bring animas, objectification, and indignity into the workplace.

Culture and climate are important. An organization that cares about having excellent culture and climate will conduct surveys at regular intervals. I have experience with Dennison surveys tracking twelve internal and external focus areas. The surveys permit targeted progress plans facilitating continuous improvement in the areas of these key enablers. However, it is important to remember that climate and culture must be accompanied by clear vision and strategy to optimize an organization.

My first flag officer job at U.S. Pacific Fleet. Our home at Pearl Harbor guarded by our faithful dogs Truman and Daisy

MENTOR AND BE MENTORED—CULTIVATE A PORTFOLIO OF MENTORS

"If you have only one mentor and he has a blind spot, you're at risk."

I should first say, my advice to junior officers was you should cultivate mentors everywhere you go. Mentors can be at the peer or near-peer level, a few years senior to you (to include senior enlisted servicemembers), and they might be very senior officers such as admirals and general officers. I also admonished that multiple mentors were a necessity, because if you have only one mentor, and he has a blind spot (or is simply misinformed), you're at risk.

The lone-mentor model is a classic single point of failure when it comes to good advice. Everyone has blind spots. Everyone has biases toward different types of duty and jobs you can pursue. Multiple mentors can help you identify and exclude poor recommendations from your solution set. I used to call it "consistent strains of advice" and when received from multiple mentors, you could rely upon a solid foundation of the mentors' counsel.

There is also the necessity to be a mentor to others. Many young naval officers believe they have nothing to offer in terms of mentorship until they accrue ten years or so in the military. Not true. Fellow peer officers, enlisted men and women, children, younger siblings can all benefit from your experiences. Now, it is important to be able to self-assess and identify "what you don't know." The reason is no advice is preferable to bad advice, so when you're just spreading your wings, it is important to know where your mentorship can add value.

One final thing I used to tell JOs is you need mentors at various stages of professional development because once they retire from service, they have expired "shelf life" and diminished value. I have been proven partially wrong on this matter. There is truth that retirees can no longer advocate officially on your behalf; however, once cultivated, the "graybeard" mentors have a wealth of time-tested information. In some cases, they have insight the modern-day senior officers simply do not have. We will see the value of staying connected to your mentors in the upcoming reflections.

Don't borrow trouble—don't worry about something until there is something to worry about—be bold

"Don't borrow trouble" was a frequent statement by my late father-in-law, a former WWII Marine, attorney, and cotton broker. Like my father, he grew up in a hard scrabble environment. But for him the challenge was not Appalachia; rather, it was the textile "mill hills" in upstate South Carolina. Don't borrow trouble was converted by me to, "Don't worry about something until there is something to worry about" when I would discuss this lesson with my cohorts in the Navy.

The idea was to sort out your priorities, identify risks, choose a course of action, and drive on. Risk awareness and mitigation are certainly important, but one can be so risk averse that they find themselves and their operations in a functional paralysis. This is especially dangerous if the person borrowing trouble is a flag or general officer. Why? If your team believes you are more scared than bold, then they are not emboldened to press forward, adapt and overcome, take calculated risk, and drive to excellence. They will not anticipate your "top cover" when they push the envelope. To be sure, you have to stay informed about the activities of your people as you don't want a team of independent operators working untethered. However, your aggressive players need to know their leadership will operate out of boldness (not fear) and stand by their efforts.

Temper your executive boldness with data

As officers become more senior, they develop more influence, and their decisions have more impact (good and bad) on the entire chain of command, associate commands, and collective mission. For this reason, applying junior officer snap decision making to senior officer or flag-level problems is dangerous. As a ground forces example, the difference between an Army officer commanding a battalion (O5 Lieutenant Colonel—leading 500) and the same officer later commanding a corps (O9 Lieutenant General—leading 20,000–40,000) is profound. A battalion commander can take a rapid assessment of a situation, apply a rudimentary level of data, issue orders, and get a "quick turn" to improve a situation. A corps commander has little opportunity for "quick turns." Moreover, the impact of corps-level decision making is far reaching, the results are slower to unfold, and a poor decision is difficult to reverse. Applying "battalion-level thinking" to a "corps-level mission" can be troublesome and potentially disastrous. Data becomes even more important as decision makers become more senior.

Beware of your rose-colored glasses and dangerous pride—find your trusted agents

As one makes admiral or general rank, it is advised by their predecessors that they will "never again have a bad meal nor hear the truth." This is the simple function of the various staff members and down echelon commands doing everything they can to present an "all is well" impression to the admiral or general in charge. FO/GOs have to somehow arrive at trusted agents to determine ground truth on the condition of their charges—especially enlisted service members. This is often done through the senior enlisted advisors (command master chief/command sergeant major) who can sidestep well-meaning but obfuscating officers trying not to "burden" the FO/GO with non-strategic issues—often referred to as "not admiral's business."

In my final flag command, I was fortunate to have outstanding staff executive assistants (mid-grade Navy and Air Force officers) who also served as keen advisors giving me a private, "on the floor" perspective about the efficacy of our leadership endeavors. An effective FO/GO must have trusted agents pulsing the culture, climate, and morale in the face of the supporting entities trying to keep the boss happy.

More dangerous than a flag officer's blind spot caused by an otherwise well-meaning staff is the occasional egomaniacal star-wearing military member or senior executive leader. The key indicator of this creature is shameless self-promotion to the exclusion of nearly all things—which may potentially include the mission itself. Such people have ceased any pretense of servant leadership. These officers build a cadre of overly loyal subordinates looking to benefit from the largess of the flag officer by feeding the self-promotion machine. These errant FO/GOs sometimes practice chaos infusion in their subordinates, so they can swoop in later to fix the problems and pick winners and losers among their minions.

The self-absorbed officers in power seek only their own advancement, and if mission accomplishment accompanies their success—fine. If not, it is the cost of achieving the higher heights. We should also recognize the loyal sycophants of the ego-driven leaders are also prone to the same misplaced practices of loyalty above all. Once a self-absorbed admiral or general is identified and sent down, the senior leaders may need to evaluate the supporting cast of the recently departed flag officer to ensure the cohorts are not infected permanently with the same malady as their former boss.

Senior officers in pinnacle positions must guard against an overdose of all-consuming pride and consider the lessons of servant leadership. We must remember: It is not about you. It is about us. It is about service and sacrifice. Senior leadership must preserve the meritocracy system of promotion for subordinates and resist the temptation to reward loyalty over all other considerations.

Purity of motive, humility and fairness are fundamental to good business. Internally, the standards of ethics and fairness inspire faith in the system of leadership accession. Externally, it is our nation's defense hanging in the balance—the protection of hearth and home. It is a primary mission of our noblest of professions—the profession of arms.

CHAPTER 13

FLAG OFFICER CONTEMPLATIONS

STAY CONNECTED TO YOUR MENTORS

I have kept in touch with my mentors who are largely retired captains and admirals given my length of service. As mentioned above, the "shelf life" for them to intervene officially on my behalf within the Navy expired on their date of retirement, but their wisdom endures. My continued relationships have often been extended friendships. With regard to one particular mentor, he completed flag assignments the same or similar to my assignments as a rear admiral. Furthermore, his post-Navy career was with a moderately sized business providing weapon systems support to the various armed forces, so his knowledge level about world events and DoD challenges was current. Periodically, he volunteered information. I paid attention, and it paid off.

My first flag position was as Director of Logistics, Fleet Supply and Ordnance (N4) for the four-star admiral who served as commander at U.S. Pacific Fleet (PACFLT). The array of challenges facing the PACFLT commander was profound and transcended eleven time zones from the U.S. West Coast into the Indian Ocean. The area of responsibility (AOR) represented a sizable portion of the world's population and four of the five perceived major national threats.

There were also expanding challenges to keep pace with growing militaries in the region and a U.S. Navy that was stretched thin. This was the first four-star officer to whom I would report directly, and the PACFLT commander's skills and experience to tackle these immense challenges were far beyond any I witnessed in three decades of service. I had my work cut out for me.

My mentor was a retired two-star Supply Corps officer who held the PACFLT N4 position at the time 9/11 took place, so he witnessed and navigated successfully some historic shifts in national policy. His advice centered upon the difficulty of command and control of logistics across the eleven time zones and the need to fashion a rapid logistics response. Through our discussions he conceived the general idea of coopting the roughly one dozen pinnacle logisticians in the PACFLT AOR. I took his general idea, and we created the PACLAC—Pacific Logistics Advisory Council. These pinnacle logisticians were the senior logistics officers assigned to the major commands in theater including:

- The two fleets in the AOR (U.S. 7th Fleet and U.S. 3rd Fleet)
- Marine Corps Forces Pacific (MARFORPAC)
- The West Coast type commanders responsible for manning, training, and equipping the aviation, surface, and submarine units in the AOR
- The task force in charge of logistics in the western Pacific (COMLOGWESTPAC)
- Commander of Defense Logistics Agency's Pacific network
- Two commanding officers serving at the Fleet Logistics Centers in Hawaii and Yokosuka, Japan

These leaders, in addition to our PACFLT staff logisticians made us a potent logistics amalgamation. Once we included the two major ordnance commands reporting to me, we then had the senior officers who controlled all commodities, products, and services (to include contract management) to support any war fight. The member officers of the PACLAC either held command or reported directly to commanding admirals or generals in the AOR. Their pinnacle status meant they held logistics decision making authority at their commands. We convened a VTC every two weeks with two general subjects— (1) upcoming near-term operations and how we could network to support, and (2) long-term planning for future combat where we might have to operate in a contested environment against a peer adversary in the region.

For the first year, we made great strides coordinating complex logistics for deployed units in the AOR, and we also were able to lay down the planning and execute many of the concept demonstrations to support potential future combat scenarios in a contested maritime environment.

During the second year, we were confronted with responding to two tragic collisions involving U.S. destroyers. Our greatest logistics challenge involved USS *John S. McCain*'s collision with *Alnic MC* in the Straits of Malacca off the coast of Malaysia. There was a collision of USS *Fitzgerald* with MV *ACX Crystal* two months before; however, *Fitzgerald*'s incident occurred in fairly close proximity to our robust naval presence at their Japanese homeport of Yokosuka. Therefore, *Fitzgerald*'s immediate logistics challenges were not as profound as McCain's.

Upon notification of *McCain*'s incident and intent for her to put into Singapore, the PACLAC assembled virtually by secure internet and phone communications. We had a member of the PACLAC resident in Singapore (a Navy captain serving as chief logistician to the commander of Logistics Group Western Pacific [COMLOGWESTPAC]). He assumed the duties as our on-scene PACLAC representative. Within a matter of hours, our PACLAC team was able to combine our cross-Pacific network with the local commands' efforts in Singapore to tackle a range of complex problems. With some heavy lifting by COMLOGWESTPAC, the 7th Fleet staff, Fleet Logistics Center Yokosuka, DLA Pacific, and Naval Munitions Command-East Asia Division, the teams were able support the ship and crew with food service and hotel accommodations which also included use of local U.S warships—most significantly the sizable amphibious assault ship USS *America* (LHA 6).[24]

In addition, arrangements were made for pier services, fresh uniforms flown in from Japan, emergency medical support, cell phones for crew communications, Wi-Fi, and initial preparations for removal of dangerous commodities including fuel and ordnance. Many of the required products and services were ready (or at least in motion) by the time the ship pulled into Singapore in the hours after the collision.

We were able to forward a rapid consolidated support summary to the Pacific Fleet commander permitting him to temporarily set aside logistics concerns and focus on the other demands for his attention—*McCain*'s crew and family members and the ship's material condition.

Without my retired mentor's recommendation and the creation of the PACLAC, we would have wasted time forming a new logistics team "on the fly" in the wake of the collision. We would have been far less responsive to the needs of the ship and crew. Instead, we were able to synchronize efforts with local commands and leverage immediately the existing and well-drilled PACLAC network to support the ship.

I sought the admiral's mentorship again at the onset of my next tour as commander of DLA Land and Maritime where we provided approximately $6 billion annually in support to Army land forces and Navy surface and subsurface forces. We had many challenges providing parts to the various Army and Marine Corps combat vehicles to include obsolescence, a thin vendor base, funding, and the task of supporting their repair depots to name a few. The Army's senior logistician to whom I provided direct support was another superb four-star officer with high standards, clear vision, and enormous capacity for detail.

My mentor once commanded a counterpart DLA organization (DLA Aviation) when he was a one-star admiral. He had similar challenges in supporting the Air Force's tactical aircraft. He had keen advice on how he aligned his command's efforts to support the services and his strategies for communicating with the Air Force senior leadership. We emulated many of the strategies, applied my own experiences, adjusted for Army-centric policies and procedures, and engaged.

I interviewed several officers who served with the senior Army official before. I determined he wanted his supporting commands to have mastery of the facts and to him that meant an understanding of every readiness driver or problem part in the Army. He also preferred one-on-one reports from supporting flag and general officers and not delegated subject matter experts from the staff.

Where we normally addressed rough orders of magnitude with senior officers, I went the other way. In our first meeting, I had in my prep binder the ability to address every contract on every troubled part in my portfolio, and these contracts numbered in the hundreds. We drove the conversation by giving him summary percentages of improvement and then self-disclosed my most difficult two or three parts contracts for each weapon system and what we were doing about it. Sometimes the solutions were switching vendors, reverse engineering, after-market research, or a number of other methods to put parts in the hands of the maintainers.

He responded well to the approach, and pressed hard for us to focus on some specific weapon systems to improve fighting readiness. Through constant consultation with our Navy, Marine Corps, and Army customers, the DLA Land and Maritime team did a fine job increasing parts availability to unprecedented heights and reducing backordered material by 18 percent. I was proud to be part of this team.

Had I not been graciously offered and accepted the advice from a longstanding mentor, my flag officer tours would have been more challenging. Remember, "the well-worn path is well worn for a reason—it works." The difference for flag and general officers is there are now fewer cohorts who have walked this particular path, so the graybeard mentors are sometimes the only ones you know who have faced this uneven ground.

A final note about mentorship: by tradition, Supply Corps officers mentor voraciously. Throughout my career, the mentorship never stopped from my first ship's SUPPOs to my retired admiral mentors, and I made every effort to give back as much good advice as I received to my junior officers.

As I was a former head detailer, mentoring became such a demand within the weekly battle rhythm I had to compartmentalize it into a single day—Friday. To my staff and Supply Corps officers seeking mentorship, it was well known they were only one Friday away from an opportunity to discuss their career questions or tour challenges by phone or in person. This was an investment of executive bandwidth to benefit junior SC officers with questions regarding service as business managers of the fleet. The mentoring sessions also kept me well informed about issues of the day and the concerns of junior officers and their families.

POLICY, SUFFICIENCY, COMPLIANCE

We covered problem solving in the senior officer chapter where one must ask the three basic questions about existence of policy, quality of policy, and compliance. These lessons also apply to admirals and generals. In my final flag billet, I served as commander of a joint duty procurement command creating and executing billions of dollars in contracts.

We had detachments collocated with the services' inventory control points, and our detachments procured complex repairable (reusable) parts on their behalf with Army, Navy, or Marine Corps funding. Because of the proximity to the service customers (and distance from my headquarters) and the funding scheme, the procurement detachments sometimes encountered suboptimal processes including poorly drafted requirements, unfunded requirements, changes in requirements far into the negotiation process, etc. The result was thousands of incomplete, unfunded, and unprioritized requirements contained within their WIP or work in process.

We applied the basic questions regarding policy existence and sufficiency discussed earlier in the book:

1. Existence of policy? Yes. Acquisition procedures and policies were abundant.
2. Quality of policy? Yes. If followed, the policies could give us high functioning organizations.
3. Are we following policy (my team and the service customer)? No.

Quite frankly, my teams were being whipsawed by competing interests, their performance suffered, and the service customers were not well served. They were getting half-baked, unfunded requirements. They were getting requirements not in their mission description—parts that, by policy, were to be bought by the services' contracting shops. They were asked to negotiate all requirements to the point of award, so the customer could select ala carte the requirements they would fund and let the other negotiations expire. In other words, the service customers desired unfunded and bad-faith negotiations on our part.

Worse than my teams' internal and external suboptimization, they were in need of some added headquarters top cover. We fixed that. We engaged the customers at all levels and stated we were going back to the basics on acquisition with the following actions:

1. We identified the parts requirements that were actually the responsibility of the services (e.g., service managed, unstable consumable items). We removed these items from our WIP and returned them to the services in keeping with policy (inter-service agreements).
2. We insisted on funded requirements. A requirement without funding is not a requirement, and we treated it as such in keeping with basic acquisition precepts (e.g., "Acquisition 101").
3. We insisted upon prioritized requirements to focus the energies of our contracting officers.
4. We instituted "roller coaster rules" with regard to negotiations (roller coaster—once you board the roller coaster and the bar comes down and the buzzer sounds, nobody gets on or off the roller coaster until the ride is through). For the contracting officers and our customers, this meant once we commenced one-on-one negotiations, the "roller coaster was in motion," and the requirement was frozen. No quantity adjustments. No requirement adjustments beyond clarifications or corrections of technical inaccuracies.

Results: we reduced WIP by three-quarters in one year. We also decreased procurement lead time to match the best performers in government contracting. The services saw the benefits of our newly reliable contracting operations collocated with their logisticians.

The mission was more efficiently executed and the warfighting servicemembers better served through improved readiness.

With Brooks visiting the Mexican tall-ship training vessel in Honolulu

MENTORSHIP MISFIRE

We discussed earlier the necessity of having a stable of multiple mentors across varying degrees of seniority. Even flag mentors can have a bias that the counsel of several other mentors can expose. I am aware of one senior officer who reportedly mentored his subordinates who were rolling to sea duty to serve on a single specific ship type exclusively. This was a binary way of looking at things and really not helpful.

There are some officers who have sufficient experience in one area such that returning to a familiar type of ship (e.g. aircraft carrier) could give the indication they lack the courage to try new things. In this particular case, the senior officer had a bias in favor of a certain type of sea service platform. I know with certainty this officer gave otherwise superb advice on other subjects, but in this case—it was suboptimal counsel.

As we mentioned earlier, the necessity for multiple mentors is critical as it mitigates the risk of a single mentor with a blind spot or bias toward or against certain career decisions. Seek the consistent strains of advice from multiple mentors, and you will be able to stay on the well-worn path to career success.

MISSED OPPORTUNITIES FOR BOLD CHANGE—"THE WORST DECISION YOU'LL EVER MAKE IS 'INDECISION'"

Patience and indecision should not be confused. Recognizing your surroundings, gathering data, getting to the 80 percent comfort zone, and then giving the go order is a good exhibition of due diligence and patience. Conversely, permitting oneself to be mired in indecision leads to organizational paralysis.

Unfortunately, we happen upon the occasional official, once promoted to admiral or general officer who develops such a cautious nature they actually paralyze their own operation. Subordinate senior officers become unsure if their efforts will be met with (1) constructive criticism and a charge to move ahead or (2) an overabundance of caution bringing the efforts to a grinding halt. Subordinate officers displaying aggression and adaptation may be met with orders to "wait until further notice"—notice that often never comes, or worse—a rebuke.

A common anecdote for such an officer is, "the staff is surprised that the officer in command took the calculated risk of driving to work every morning considering their proclivity for caution." A flag/general officer or senior executive cannot be so fearful for their job they fail to do their job. "Holding serve" for a tour as a senior leader—especially an admiral or general in command—is a waste of time, resources, and a valuable promotion that could have gone to someone more up to the task.

BOLD DECISION THAT LACKED SUFFICIENT DATA

As a first-time, O5 commanding officer, I observed a commander of a large logistics organization issue an idle statement about the location of an overseas operation supporting combat in nearby Iraq.

He said, "I would like to see this support command and their products moved closer to the fight." The fight existed in Iraq, and this was a bold and intuitively obvious idea—especially from a ground forces perspective. As such, the commanding general's subordinate staff proceeded to issue orders to move the smaller detachment from one foreign nation to another without applying data to determine the after effects. The result was a movement of the preponderance of the support detachment and commodities one country nearer to Iraq (290 miles closer).

Several problems ensued:

1. The old position of the support command and its products were next to a well-established aviation logistics node (air strip) where there existed frequent air logistics channel flights directly into Iraq. The new location, although physically closer, had less frequent air access into Iraq for logistics, so the flow of material for most customers was actually slowed by the move.
2. The manpower at the old location was U.S. military, and as such, inexpensive from a touch labor perspective. The manpower at the new location was contracted labor utilizing third country nationals (TCNs are immigrant labor [not U.S. and not from the hosting country]). TCNs were typically from countries in South East Asia, and these contracted TCNs were more expensive per transaction by magnitudes than the U.S. military members in the old location.
3. The TCNs were not cleared to handle classified material (a significant subset to the product line and logistics mission); therefore, only a portion of the products could be moved to the new location.
4. TCNs aside, the contracted facility at the new location did not have storage facilities suitable for classified material nor the required reaction force necessary if a break-in occurred.

So, even if we were somehow able to shift the U.S. military from the old location to the new location (a major task requiring

Department of State and DoD involvement), the new facilities were unsuitable to the classified portion of the mission.

We wound up with a hybrid/Frankenstein model—a dual operation with unclassified material in the new location handled by expensive TCNs and the classified mission retained in the old location handled by the U.S. military members. So, the end result of a three-star's idle comment (that was executed without further study or advice from his immediate subordinates) was: A movement of only a portion of the products to a location (though closer physically) that was further away logistically (via air nodes), much more expensive by transaction, and slower in response time overall.

In fact, air shipments from the new location were sometimes routed through the older location's associated air node on the way to Iraq. In short, the team suboptimized the process. They executed an idle comment as an order—without sufficient study, and they lacked the wherewithal to approach the three-star commander with applicable data to refute the assumed benefits of the "bold idea." Boldness is an absolute necessity as a senior commander, yet the application of supporting data is a critical catalyst to the process of confirming a "bold idea" is a "wise decision."

REMEMBER THE TWENTY-TWO

There have been many articles regarding the epidemic of veteran and active-duty suicide. Over the past decade, several publications have identified a suicide rate of twenty-two current and former military members per day.[25] The causes are many and sometimes include PTSD; however, it is prevention we will highlight. I had only indirect exposure to suicide for most of my career. For example, we had at least one Sailor or Marine jump over the side on all four of the ships on which I served. The ship's crew and air detachments were able to recover all but one. Still, I had a false sense of security in my ability as a leader as none of the suicide attempts at any of my units were my Sailors. I mistakenly believed I had an appropriate climate and leadership network which rendered us immune to the possibility of suicide.

It was not until my first command tour when I was confronted directly with suicide. One of distribution depots under my command had nine retail offices around the world. At one isolated office overseas, a young Sailor attempted suicide. It was not a cry for help; rather, he meant to take his own life. Only an observant petty officer and some fast action by the team and first responders saved the day. For me, I had not met the youngster—he had not yet reported during my most recent periodic visit a few months prior.

I took the first phone call, spoke with the detachment OIC, quickly gathered as much initial information (including the five Ws because remember, the first story is never the story), and we made the required reports up the chain of command. I also had the duty to phone the Sailor's parents, advise them of the situation, and give them details about what we were doing to care for their son. It was a tough conversation as one might imagine. In the end, we obtained for the Sailor some initial care overseas. He was then returned to a U.S. military hospital, and he recovered.

However, in reviewing the case, our "after action report" revealed the young Sailor was a loner, and he was unhappy at the overseas location. He showed these and other signs that although mild, were indicators we should have recognized. We didn't. I then thought back throughout my career to all the Sailors I could recall who attempted suicide on ships and ashore.

I remembered reading the after action reports and lessons learned, and then it hit me. There were ALWAYS signs. They were often subtle such as changes in personality, marital stress, financial woes, deployment events, etc. We were sometimes surprised, but when we dug into the details—the signs were there. We needed to do a better job detecting the signs and addressing the issues. We needed to get to know our people better. We needed better internal communication in this matter.

I served another fourteen years after this first close call with the Sailor under my charge. Going forward—at every unit in which I served or commanded, we discussed Sailor pace and balance, and signs of struggle with great frequency. To borrow a sonar term—we went "active" instead of "passive." We made some good and necessary intercessions. Sometimes we surprised a Sailor with our concern, but in balance, the Sailors knew we cared enough to ask some probing questions.

It was a net-positive, even when we were wrong owing to our abundance of caution. The big lesson to be learned: There are ALWAYS signs. We must train and prepare our leadership and family members to look, listen, and ASK our service members past and present the polite and probing questions, so we can apply assistance when needed. We need to open our eyes to the "twenty-two" among us.

EXECUTION OF STRATEGY—ALIGNMENT OF EFFORT

In my last command, we were part of a network of logistics commands providing approximately $40 billion in products and services to the U.S. Armed Forces and other federal entities (e.g., DoD, FEMA, Department of Homeland Security, Department of State, etc.). My team's annual contribution was approximately $4 billion (not counting our Army/Navy repairable parts support). Our agency director did a really fine job of aligning efforts through a strategic plan with annual updates, yearly requirements for subordinate supporting plan development, and twice annual visits to the subordinate commands to receive briefs and provide comment and direction.

The visits called "dynamic operating plan reviews" were a good example of a "show up" strategy, and they also served as a checkup on progress. Measurable end states of milestones in support of the strategic plan were a heavy focus. The agency director asked the questions: What are you doing? How do you know you're making progress? What adjustments to the plans should be made? Are you aligned with the latest version of the strategic plan?

In addition to the alignment check, it also provided the director the opportunity to meet people in the subordinate commands, hold town halls, and get out into the spaces. This served as an occasion for sensing climate and morale at the supporting locations and to confirm or refute past climate surveys which were done formally every two years.

This is a fine example of complex strategic planning, transition from long-term goals to near-term actions, a "show up—inspect/expect" scheme to keep all major subordinate commands in alignment, and optimization of command and control. These methods were very effective in the administration of a $40 billion agency with 26,000 associates.

CHAPTER 14

ENDURING THEMES

There are some themes that have stood firm throughout my years as they were informed by the farm, schools, our family, and a career in the Navy. Some of the experiences simply reinforced the lessons from my childhood. Some were discoveries made by my wife and me during our three decades of marriage. Some are incidents in life that will stay with me as long as memory serves. A short list is outlined in this chapter.

WORK IS STILL WORK—SO GET TO WORK

The work never goes away. Certainly, the nature of the work changes, but the demand for work does not. I sometimes have encountered professionals who think that with promotion comes the latitude to slack off. I have heard it said no one gets promoted with the expectation they will do less. In the professional world, corporations do not pay associates six-figure salaries to go home at 3 p.m. You are still under the burden of adding value. Recommendations: refresh the time management skills. Set the goals. Set the pace. Set the example. In short: get to work.

PERPETUAL EDUCATION

As outlined earlier, the importance of education was a daily drumbeat from my parents. Mom was a teacher, and Dad always pressed home the value of education. This message was passed on to multiple generations. Dad never went to college, but his kids did, and so did his grandchildren. He continued the communication tradition with his grandchildren that he and Mother started over a half-century earlier with my brother, sister, and me.

Although not a college man, Dad took great pride in the educational achievements of his progeny. At his death, he had an array of college stickers on the back of his car—one for each school attended by his six grandchildren. They all graduated college in either four or five years' time and have fine careers ahead of them. They also had words of their grandparents echoing in their ears as they went off to school: "Get your books."

Dad's last car—a Buick with his grandkids' colleges represented

ORDERS AND ETHICS ARE STILL IN FORCE

With greater seniority, some leaders assume their increased scope and scale of responsibilities is accompanied by a sliding scale permitting them to operate under a lower standard of ethics.

Invariably, some of this malfeasance is uncovered, and the offending officers are relieved and shamed publicly. What these officers are unwilling to understand is they failed the basic test of an official's original charter—willingness to follow orders as they relate to ethical standards.

Far from the more egregious violations found in a Fat Leonard type of scandal, these disgraced officers are guilty typically of more benign offenses such as travel violations or public embarrassment from overindulgence in alcohol. This is also a situation where one's past hard work, high achievement, and pinnacle promotion might become mixed with sinful pride forming a witch's brew of trouble and tragedy. These senior officials presume an executive pass for their missteps because of their perceived station and importance.

Bottom line: the processes are unchanged. The standard is the same. At a very basic level, you are still in the business of following orders—now in the form of policy and regulations. An unwillingness or inability to follow orders is a breach of trust. Any breach of trust, no matter how minor, calls into question an officer's willingness to subject themselves to rules and regulations applicable to all.

An officer breaking faith on a lower level is presumed to have the same proclivity when engaged in operations of greater responsibility. Senior officials are expected to know better. Once trust is lost, you're on the way out the door. Stay true to core values, uphold the standard, and remember: retirement with honor is a full-time job.

STAY FIT

Fitness is a condition of employment for military members, and it is also a quality-of-life issue and stress reliever for corporate counterparts. In the military, aging officers must continue to meet high standards of fitness and readiness. Why? First, it is a fundamental tenant of leadership by example. Second, you will look better, and our present and potential future antagonists are watching. You want to confirm their suspicion that all members of the U.S. military are prepared to engage across the entire range of military operations and defeat all threats. A sharp and fit personal appearance reinforces this impression.

Finally, your subordinates want to know the boss—"the old man" in my case—has the strength and stamina to pull his or her own weight in a deployed environment. Senior leaders cannot permit themselves to become the weak link—especially when service in a combat environment is a potential eventuality. Corpulent and unfit senior officers suffer a loss in credibility through the hypocrisy that stems from their lack of fitness. Hit the gym.

KEEPING THE FAITH

It should be clear that faith was a persistent theme in my childhood, and my interaction with the church started earlier than one might expect. I was baptized by our parish priest the day after my birth as I was due to have emergent surgery before I was fully one day old. The medical procedure was a success, and my day-one baptism marked my entry into my family's faith voyage for which our mother was the ship's captain and Christ is the north star. Mom led by example and ensured faith was at the forefront of her children's lives. Her childhood church was to be our church, and Good Shepherd Episcopal in Lexington was as much a home to us as our farm in Avon. Faith has continued to be a driving force in my professional service as a Naval officer as well as my in family duties as a husband and father. I am blessed to have a wife who participates enthusiastically in this all-important part of my life.

As discussed, my first ship was pulled out of the shipyards and deployed to Desert Shield/Storm in a little over a week. As one might expect, we leaned heavily on our chaplains as the ship departed on a wartime deployment. I sought out the protestant chaplains on board USS *Guam* to attend services, but they were somewhat foreign to me as my Episcopalian background was more liturgical. I approached the ship's senior chaplain, a Navy captain/Roman Catholic priest who began his service in Vietnam. We already had a great relationship, and he was a force multiplier for our Sailors on the ship knowing "when to hug 'em and when to slug 'em." He could comfort a young Sailor or Marine who lost a family member as easily as he could appeal to the pride of a youngster who was facing fear for the first time.

As he was Roman Catholic, I asked him if I could attend his services since they were closer in liturgical structure to my Episcopal experience. This is a tall order for a Roman Catholic priest to grant communion to a non-Catholic—many do not. I asked. He said, "Sure." And then as we were walking down the passageway toward the ship's chapel, he said: "John, I gotta ask—any chance of you going RC?" I smiled and said, "No sir." He chuckled and said, "I didn't think so, but I had to ask." We had a good laugh that day. He proved especially important to our surprise mission called Operation Eastern Exit involving the rescue of 281 refugees from Somalia just before the commencement of the air war (discussed later).

My interaction with the USS *Guam*'s chaplain started a long series of great relationships with Navy chaplains and laypersons on ships and ashore throughout my career. I was never refused a spiritual accommodation for me or any of my Sailors or Marines. My last experience with the Chaplain Corps was during our initial admiral tour in Hawaii. Our neighbor and friend in Oahu was assigned as the Pacific Fleet chaplain. He was a Texas farmer—I was a Kentucky farmer. We had a lot in common, and our wives also hit it off. He was another great American chaplain who devoted his life to his faith and his nation's service as he ministered to Sailors and Marines around the world wherever they were stationed—no matter the danger.

My wife and I have also been exceedingly well served by civilian Episcopal and Anglican clergy wherever we were stationed. We liked to participate actively in outreach committees. Also, I was appointed or elected to the church vestry at two Episcopal parishes over the years. We still keep up with two of the parish priests to this day, and they have always been available to help me as well as my family even after we moved away from their churches. In fact, one of these gentlemen showed up at my father's hospital bed in Kentucky when he was sick in his waning years.

As Mother always said: "When tough times are upon you, give it up to the Lord," and that is some good advice. To be sure, my family and I have not wanted for religious support in our dozen locations in which we have lived. In the COVID-19 crisis, I was especially impressed with our Anglican parish in Ohio and their courageous and innovative ways to reach the congregation virtually, administer the sacraments safely, and keep the ties that bind. Thanks to all and God bless.

My hometown church—The Episcopal Church of the Good Shepherd in Lexington, Kentucky, and the dedication plaque located inside

FAMILY COMMUNICATIONS ARE ALL-IMPORTANT

We have seen the ever-increasing importance of communication throughout the book. Remember, communication is "the root of all evil when you do not have enough, and it cures all ills when you apply more." This is especially true with one's family. I began my career by shielding my wife and small children from the machinations within the Navy because I did not want to burden them with my challenges.

This was a poor strategy. First, I had difficulty tackling my professional problems alone—without a loving and trustworthy sounding board. Second, I mistakenly believed Brooks and our children might have difficulty understanding the nature of my business. Finally, I did not realize the benefit greater information flow would bring to our entire family. I made it through my first two tours with limited Navy communications to the family. My third tour was on a guided missile frigate, and the job proved too tough to navigate privately.

I began confiding in my wife about the struggles on board the ship, what we were doing to fix the problems, the reasons for the extended working hours, and new complications discovered along the way. Brooks was a quick study and a thoughtful counselor as I brought my troubles home. The results were cathartic for me. The act of divulging my job activities to Brooks was a great stress reliever. As a result, I began to share more with Brooks and the kids.

We perfected the "Navy family" discussions, and I soon saw the advantages for Brooks and our children. Throughout our tours, I related to the family the nature of my job and all the things good and bad that could happen over the next few years including shortened tours or tour extensions, assignments in places we might not anticipate or want, unpredicted deployments for me, and family separation in general.

I found the best opportunity for family communications about the Navy was during meals. I realized one major benefit was I was conditioning my family over time to the sometimes unfortunate disappointments of Navy life. The results were dramatic. When I would arrive at home with news of a future move, I would get the sunk cost of angst accompanying any big change. However, because I repeatedly discussed these possibilities in the past, my wife and our children quickly transitioned into a team working on an upcoming move. In no time, we were gathering information about new neighborhoods, homes, places of employment, schools, sports teams, and churches. We were productively working the challenge of the next move—as a team—even if it was sometimes to a less than desired location.

Later I served as the head detailer for the Supply Corps as a captain. I observed some officers who tried to keep their families in the dark about the Navy and an officer's hurdles in the service. These officers often engendered family mutinies when they brought suboptimal news to spouses and children at home. I believe the reason was that the officers' family members were not habituated to the idea of the needs of the Navy pushing the them to a place different than they anticipated. The well-meaning officers wanted to spare their families the stress of the unknown. However, the families kept in the dark were unprepared mentally to handle these situations.

The cure for this ill was frequent, open, and honest family communications. I have mentored young officers on this subject at every opportunity. I recommend the discussions occur nightly at the dinner table. Increased communications at home were fundamental to my ability to keep Brooks and our children updated, engaged, and actively involved in overcoming the obstacles inherent to military life. I have no doubt open communications can assist all military members to acclimate their families to the stresses of service in the U.S. Armed Forces. I believe this is a tool of equal value for high-stress civilians as well. While good communications were important to my professional success, they were all-important to the health and welfare of my family.

HARD WORK AND A POSITIVE ATTITUDE—"YOU NEED ONLY LOOK ACROSS THE STREET TO SEE HOW BLESSED YOU ARE."

Like my father, my father-in-law came from a tough childhood in Upstate South Carolina. I am told that as a child, his family home burned a few days before Christmas one year. He and his siblings spent a long time scattered about with relatives while another home could be found so the family could be reconstituted. He was a World War II Marine from the Pacific theater, he put himself through college (GI bill) and law school after the war, and he and his wife raised five fine children.

If circumstances dictated, he could be tough, but otherwise he had a heart of gold. He used to say there were always people in far worse condition than we were, and we needed only to "look across the street" to see how blessed we were. He knew this to be true because he lived it—as a child. He possessed an infectious positive attitude, and he reminded me of my dad. I took his advice and modified it a little telling my Sailors: "Life is too short to have a bad day, so don't let yourself have a bad day."

The choice is yours. A positive attitude is rocket fuel in any organization. It is a constructive contagion. People gravitate to the positive entities, and they avoid the curmudgeons. When all else fails—keep charging ahead, stay positive, and look to the bright side—because there is always a bright side. Look across the street sometime. You will probably see that life for you is pretty good, and it will put today's problems into perspective.

THINGS BIGGER THAN YOURSELF PART I: OPERATION EASTERN EXIT

My first ship was USS *Guam* (LPH 9). As outlined previously, we deployed on short notice to Desert Shield (preparation for the Gulf War) followed by Desert Storm (Gulf War). By then I was promoted from ensign to lieutenant (junior grade), and I transitioned from my first position as S-8 material officer to S-6 (aviation support officer). This job was important in that our ship type (LPH—landing platform helicopter) had no well-deck and associated amphibious vehicles to ferry our 1,200 Marines through the water ashore for combat. Rather, we depended solely on the twenty-four embarked CH-46 Sea Knight (medium-lift) helicopters to execute our mission.

I was lucky to have the services of an ace petty officer in the division who would later promote to chief petty officer. We embarked our Marines and aircraft and sailed east to the north Arabian Sea in preparation to enter the Persian Gulf to participate in the war. Sandwiched between Desert Shield (buildup for the war) and Desert Storm (execution of the war), we participated in Operation Eastern Exit—the rescue from the U.S. Embassy in Mogadishu, Somalia of 281 people from thirty-two countries including twelve ambassadors or *chargés d'affaires*.

We were steaming in the North Arabian Sea with the other ships in the Amphibious Task Force. After issuance of emergency distress from the U.S. ambassador to Somalia, our ship, in company with USS *Trenton*, was ordered south toward Mogadishu at high speed. Long-range, heavy-lift helicopters were dispatched with Marines and SEALs to secure the embassy grounds from surrounding warring factions.

The Marines and SEALs held the embassy overnight in anticipation of more medium-lift helicopters to evacuate the refugees the next morning. The ships and rescue helicopters arrived off the coast the next day to launch and recover the evacuees. Our team on the ground had to do some fast talking with the local warlords who were threatening to shoot down the rescuing helicopters. By the time the warlords were ready to shoot, the last aircraft took off bringing our people home.

The helicopters brought the evacuees to us in waves. Every time the aircraft elevator was lowered from the flight deck to the hangar, we saw the eyes of people who had been through quite an ordeal. The 281 people were sheltering on the embassy grounds—ducking gunfire from outside the embassy walls for days, and they were exhausted, dirty, and hungry. Sailors and Marines donated their uniforms to serve as clean clothing, and the ship soon took on the look of an episode of *Gilligan's Island* with civilians wearing our uniforms any way they pleased. The ships began serving meals, making space for families and individuals to sleep, and providing medical care. A pregnant woman gave birth through caesarean section by the Navy doctors and nurses on board.

We received orders to deliver the evacuees to Muscat, Oman. I was assigned as ambassadors' liaison seeing they had all communications and material necessary to conduct business while on the way to Oman. Needless to say, the ambassadors and chargés d'affaires had much to communicate to their home countries. I had the pleasure of attending meetings and meals with these senior representatives and observed the ambassadors/charges from countries such as USA, USSR, UK, Kenya, UAE, Sudan, Turkey, Nigeria, Oman, Kuwait, Qatar, and Germany. They coexisted congenially while politely cutting each other to pieces in civil debate. It was a tremendous experience to see the transformation of hungry and tired people in need of rescue to happy, healthy, and grateful citizens returned to safety.

USS *Guam* (LPH 9) "Swift and Bold"[26]

While this was certainly not what I envisioned as an ensign when I commissioned into the Navy in 1988, the 1991 rescue was quite fulfilling. Eastern Exit was a classic non-combat evacuation operation (NEO), but it was dwarfed by the air war which commenced shortly thereafter. As such, I have heard Eastern Exit described as "the best operation you never heard of." For our part, each Sailor and Marine received a letter in their service record extolling the ". . . daring, swift, gallant, and humanitarian rescue of two hundred eighty-one souls . . ." signed by the twelve ambassadors and chargés d'affaires who were also rescued.[27]

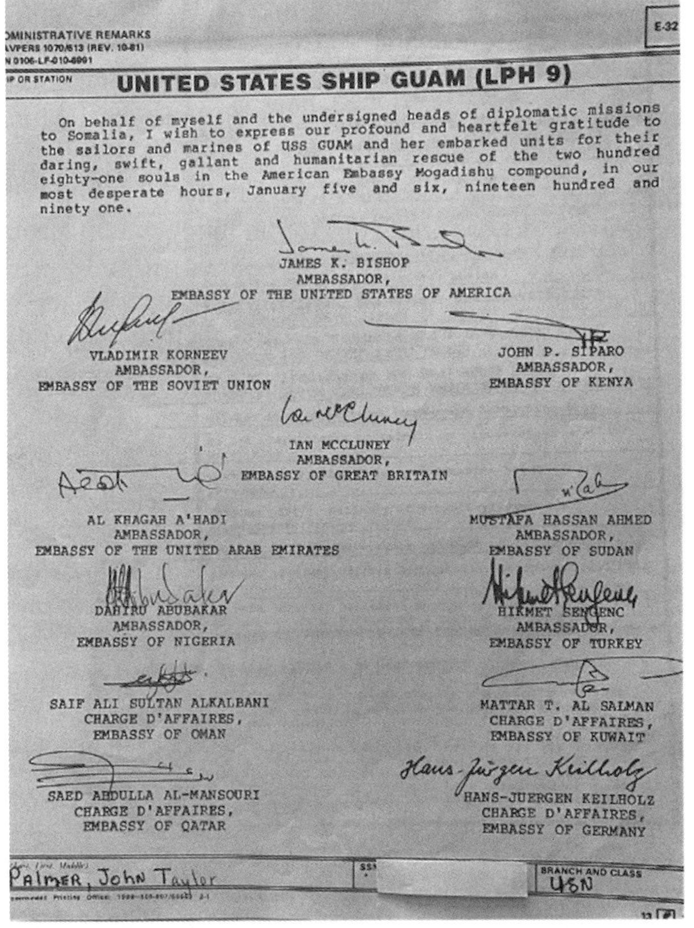

ADMINISTRATIVE REMARKS
NAVPERS 1070/613 (REV. 10-81)
SN 0106-LF-010-6991

E-32

SHIP OR STATION **UNITED STATES SHIP GUAM (LPH 9)**

On behalf of myself and the undersigned heads of diplomatic missions to Somalia, I wish to express our profound and heartfelt gratitude to the sailors and marines of USS GUAM and her embarked units for their daring, swift, gallant and humanitarian rescue of the two hundred eighty-one souls in the American Embassy Mogadishu compound, in our most desperate hours, January five and six, nineteen hundred and ninety one.

JAMES K. BISHOP
AMBASSADOR,
EMBASSY OF THE UNITED STATES OF AMERICA

VLADIMIR KORNEEV
AMBASSADOR,
EMBASSY OF THE SOVIET UNION

JOHN P. SIPARO
AMBASSADOR,
EMBASSY OF KENYA

IAN MCCLUNEY
AMBASSADOR,
EMBASSY OF GREAT BRITAIN

AL KHAGAH A'HADI
AMBASSADOR,
EMBASSY OF THE UNITED ARAB EMIRATES

MUSTAFA HASSAN AHMED
AMBASSADOR,
EMBASSY OF SUDAN

DAHIRU ABUBAKAR
AMBASSADOR,
EMBASSY OF NIGERIA

HIKMET SENGENC
AMBASSADOR,
EMBASSY OF TURKEY

SAIF ALI SULTAN ALKALBANI
CHARGE D'AFFAIRES,
EMBASSY OF OMAN

MATTAR T. AL SALMAN
CHARGE D'AFFAIRES,
EMBASSY OF KUWAIT

SAED ABDULLA AL-MANSOURI
CHARGE D'AFFAIRES,
EMBASSY OF QATAR

Hans-Jürgen Keilholz
HANS-JUERGEN KEILHOLZ
CHARGE D'AFFAIRES,
EMBASSY OF GERMANY

PALMER, John Taylor | SSN | BRANCH AND CLASS USN

Service record entry for *Guam* crew containing a note of thanks from ambassadors and chargés d'affaires rescued during Eastern Exit

THINGS BIGGER THAN YOURSELF PART II: 9/11 AND NYC—OPERATION NOBLE EAGLE

The nuclear-powered aircraft carrier USS *George Washington* (CVN 73) was my third ship, my first aircraft carrier, and my first ship on which I served as a lieutenant commander or senior officer. Note: Technically the Navy doesn't designate you as "senior" and permit you to wear the gold braided "brass hat" until you reach full commander (O5), but the other services and joint doctrine consider lieutenant commanders (O4) as "senior" along with their service counterparts—USA, USMC, and USAF majors.

I served as principal assistant for logistics (PAL, for short), and I was in charge of the divisions controlling parts, budget, contracting, materiel, and the all-important logistics/transportation pipeline from the U.S. to wherever the ship happened to be located in the world.

In September of 2001, we had just completed a shipyard maintenance period and were underway doing independent steaming to refresh our basic skills (routine damage control, propulsion, maneuvering, communications, and ship's services). We were without the ship's embarked airwing of seventy-five aircraft as our flight deck was yet to be certified for accommodating the wing. As such, we had little ordnance and minimal aircraft fuel (JP-5) on board.

On the morning of September 11, we were steaming off the Virginia Capes. We could see news communications throughout the ship by way of satellite transmission, and we observed the first tower strike on TV. It looked to most to be a terrible accident by an errant pilot. When the second tower was struck, we knew immediately something more sinister was occurring. Our TV news feed was immediately turned off by the ship's CO, so we could focus on the rapidly unfolding tasks at hand.

We could feel the ship accelerate to high speed, and we turned north. Our CO addressed the crew saying we were going to support the situation in New York. Subsequently, word got out about the Pentagon strike and the aircraft crash in Pennsylvania. We knew we were in a state of war. The announcement was made: "Prepare to recover aircraft!" The air department team rigged our uncertified deck to "trap" incoming aircraft (facilitate tailhook landings) as they made ready the arresting gear (for landing) and catapults for future launches.

In a few short hours, we were joined by a small complement of armed aircraft from the USS *John F. Kennedy* airwing. The aircraft consisted mainly of tactical Naval aircraft and airborne early warning aircraft for radar detection and command and control (C2) of flights in New York air space.

We received direction that stemmed from a request ostensibly from the governor's office asking that *Washington* pull close enough to New York City for the inhabitants to see us and take some comfort in the presence of the ship and aircraft. We did so, but the close-in sailing track also gave all on board a view of the smoke columns from the location where the Twin Towers stood just one day earlier.

An aerial photo was snapped that shows the ship with lower Manhattan on the horizon. The firsthand images seared into our memories the events of 9/11. We were angry, and I personally felt some level of guilt that we let this happen to our innocent citizens. We spent several days guarding New York City's air space in conjunction with several shore-based commands from our joint forces in an operation later dubbed Noble Eagle.[28]

We knew the world was forever changed. We did not know if/when we would go home. There was much speculation we would receive our combat stores at sea, embark our aircraft, and head east to war. As it stood, we went back to Norfolk about seven days later. As I drove to visit my family living at that time in Richmond, I had never seen so many American flags. Every home and nearly every car was adorned with flags, yellow ribbons, handwritten messages on signs and windows. The U.S. was united in a manner I had not seen before nor since, and we had a changed world before us.

As for *Washington* and Carrier Air Wing 17, we conducted training and workups, and we deployed to do our part in Operation Enduring Freedom by conducting air strikes in southwest Asia in 2002. For the remainder of my time on board *George Washington*, we were the ship New Yorkers remembered seeing on the horizon providing some small measure of peace of mind in the midst of chaos.

We were frequently the hosts for visitors from New York for memorials and expressions of gratitude, and we received countless letters from our neighbors to the north. Along with *Guam*'s rescue in Eastern Exit, I engaged in a second act as a Naval officer I never anticipated—the task of protecting an American city after the deadly terrorist attacks.

Many past lessons were employed, and future lessons learned in this operation. Certainly, one must be prepared to transition to a combat posture at all times, even in the previously presumed safe environment of the continental United States. Adaptability is key. Given our recent operational downtime for maintenance and our position in the training cycle, we were not perceived to be a combat-ready asset on the morning of 9/11. Still, we had to find a way to get there—to perform, and we did. Our world can transform forever in a single event. September 11 was our generation's stock market crash—our Pearl Harbor—our presidential assassination. We haven't been and will never be the same as we were on September 10. For us in the profession of arms, it was a time to atone for letting the bad guys inside our wire. It was time for us to do our part to set things right and make sure it never happened again.

On board USS *George Washington* (CVN 73) on the morning of September 12, 2001 off NYC—smoke from the Twin Towers in the background[29]

THINGS BIGGER THAN YOURSELF PART III: JOINT TASK FORCE KATRINA

On my final ship, *Harry S. Truman*, I followed an outstanding officer as the ship's Supply Officer who went on to a distinguished career and achieved flag rank. The ship's CO was skeptical of the new "SUPPO," and I could tell I had not yet established credibility with him after taking over. Still the CO was a hard-driving and imminently fair man commanding one of our nation's most precious military assets. A tragedy soon provided an opportunity for our team to display our acumen and become an indispensable player as we talked about earlier in the book.

The ship was in Norfolk, Virginia, during an in-port period. Hurricane Katrina struck Gulf Coast Louisiana and Mississippi, and we received orders to sail to the Gulf of Mexico to provide relief as soon as possible. My team (the ship's supply department) first contacted our higher echelon—the type commander's staff. We asked for any logistics lessons learned from the aircraft carrier *Abraham Lincoln* that responded to Asian tsunami victims the previous year.

With the *Lincoln*'s after action report (AAR) in hand, we called a meeting with our principal assistants and their ten supply department division officers and chief petty officers (senior enlisted). We used the *Lincoln* AAR as a starting point to make immediate decisions on what to order and load out. After one hour, we had a plan and departed the meeting to execute the procurement of ship's supplies to support the crew on deployment as well as tons of food, meals-ready-to-eat (MREs), water, empty water bottles (nuclear-powered ships make a lot of fresh water suitable for bottling and sending), tents, bedding, first aid supplies, lights, batteries, slings, tarps, and more.

A few hours later, I received a call to the captain's cabin so he might provide direction on what he believed we should have on board for the deployment. I quickly laid out our communications with the type commander, the materiel ordered, items already loaded, and stores still scheduled to be loaded plus the *Lincoln* report and our additional action items we derived in our supply department planning session.

The CO was pleasantly surprised that we were not only far ahead, but we were a half-day away from being completely loaded from a logistics and humanitarian relief perspective. The result was we procured and loaded seventy-three tons of material to support an expedited underway in forty-eight hours. We deployed as part of Joint Task Force Katrina and in company with other ships, we provided much-needed relief to U.S. citizens who were facing extreme challenges in the hurricane's wake.[30] Personally, as the newly arrived ship's senior logistician, I was provided the opportunity to deliver a confidence booster to our CO. Our JTF Katrina performance seemed to ease any question his mind about the new SUPPO and *Truman*'s supply department.

USS *Harry S. Truman* (CVN 75) during underway replenishment[31]

This was the third and final humanitarian event in which I participated as a Naval officer. Nearly nine of my thirty-two years of service were at sea. There are many moments from which I derive pride and satisfaction, but Operations Eastern Exit, Noble Eagle, and Joint Task Force Katrina are at or near the top of the list. Reflecting upon my upbringing and training, these represent "old and gray" memories I will carry with me always. These operations also reinforced the premise that team goals were bigger than any individual concerns as we executed missions more than war, helping those less fortunate, and making a difference in the lives of those we did not know—those whom we would not likely see again.

CHAPTER 15

FROM NAVY TO CIVILIAN

I spent my career as a logistician in the Supply Corps, and it was very rewarding. Certainly, the Supply Corps' heavy operational nature meant these "business managers of the fleet" were ever-present on deployments afloat and ashore downrange. From a macro perspective, logistics have been the key enabler to U.S. military victories since the Civil War. After 9/11, much of my Naval service was focused on the war on terror. For our part, logistics was again vital to our nation's success as we strove to contain the terrorist bad guys after the terrorist attacks.

Our unique ability to position and sustain our joint forces around the world—to replenish and rearm our naval units while underway permitted our military to keep the bad guys in the bad guy box on the other side of the planet until they either changed their ways or clearance was given to engage and take them out. The impact was clear. We kept much of the terrorist threat away from our shores, and that is a legacy about which servicemembers from my era can be proud.

After thirty-two years, I retired from the Navy in the fall of 2020. This was at the height of COVID-19, and I was worried about the pandemic impact on the job market for me. I was thankful for my career as a logistician as much of my experience was applicable to civilian businesses. We decided to move to my wife's hometown, the same town where my son, his wife, and two of our four grandchildren reside. I focused my employment efforts on upstate South Carolina industry, but I was blessed to receive a wonderful opportunity to serve as company CEO for a newly established corporation in Detroit, Michigan. Having only been serving a few months in this capacity, I have just begun to accumulate firsthand lessons about the differences between military service and corporate service.

My retirement "Shadow Box" displaying career history, command coins and ship's patches among other artifacts

Regardless, military members considering retirement should not take for granted the intrinsic benefits of uniformed service.

Public admiration for our armed forces is preeminent in the United States. The purity of motive and mission is, for me, unique to our profession of arms. Corporate culture and norms are somewhat different than those found in government service, but that is what makes this new adventure exciting. Some constants are still present. There is always a mission. There are always goals. There are always challenges.

Brooks is back in business as a registered nurse working at the local hospital, and she is also watching our two youngest grandchildren on a fixed schedule. We are seeing family more often than ever before in South Carolina. Thankfully, we are only a half-day's drive from our other child, her husband, and our two older grandchildren. In short, we're both employed, we are near family for the first time in our married lives, and we are blessed beyond description. Yet, the lessons from the farm and the Navy inform our daily activity and how we attack new challenges. I'm adding new corporate lessons and leadership tools to my tool kit every day. More on that in the future.

ABOUT THE AUTHOR

Rear Admiral (retired) John Palmer is a native of Lexington, Kentucky. He is married to the former Elizabeth Brooks Mahaffey (Brooks) of Spartanburg, South Carolina. They are the proud parents of two children—Elizabeth Palmer Sanders and John Taylor Palmer Jr. They are blessed with four grandchildren. The Palmers live among family in Spartanburg where Brooks works as a registered nurse.

The author is a graduate of The Citadel, The Military College of South Carolina earning a bachelor of science degree in business administration. He is also a graduate of the Naval Postgraduate School holding a master of science degree in systems management (acquisition and contract management) and the Columbia University Graduate School of Business senior executive program.

The Palmers served over thirty-two years as a Navy family with the author retiring at the rank of rear admiral. His Navy career included nearly nine years at sea while assigned to four ships. In addition, he was entrusted with command during three tours leading four units spanning six years. He commanded subordinate operations in over a dozen overseas locations. During his naval career, Admiral Palmer earned several warfare and professional qualifications and is entitled to wear various personal, unit, and service awards including the Defense Superior Service Medal and Combat Action Ribbon.

The author serves presently as chief executive officer of UVSheltron, Inc. located in Pontiac, Michigan. UVSheltron designs and manufactures ultraviolet light devices used for disinfection of rooms and objects of harmful pathogens as well as purification of air in common spaces. Admiral Palmer also participates in management of family farms in Kentucky, and he is founder and owner of JT Palmer Enterprises, LLC located in Spartanburg.

BIBLIOGRAPHY

Bomboy, Scott. "Lincoln and Taney's great writ showdown," Constitution Daily, National Constitution Center, Philadelphia, PA (May 28, 2021). https://constitutioncenter.org/blog/lincoln-and-taneys-great-writ-showdown.

Campbell, Photographer's Mate Third Class J. Scott. September 12, 2001, New York City. https://commons.wikimedia.org/wiki/File:US_Navy_010912-N-1407C-001_USS_George_Washington_(CVN_73).jpg.

Cooke, Edmund Vance. "How Did You Die," Allpoetry.com. https://allpoetry.com/How-Did-You-Die-.

Conroy, Pat. *The Lords of Discipline*. New York: Random House, Inc., 1980.

Horn, Joshua. "Was Sherman a War Criminal?" Discerning History (December 16, 2014). http://discerninghistory.com/2014/12/was-sherman-a-war-criminal/.

Department of the Navy (Office of the Chief of Naval Operations). "Report on the Collision between USS FITZGERALD (DDG 62) and Motor Vessel ACX CRYSTAL" and "Report on the Collision between USS JOHN S MCCAIN (DDG 56) and Motor Vessel ALNIC MC," (October 23, 2017), 1–71. https://s3.amazonaws.com/CHINFO/USS+Fitzgerald+and+USS+John+S+McCain+Collision+Reports.pdf.

Haiken, Melanie. "Suicide Rate Among Vets and Active Duty Military Jumps—Now 22 a Day," Forbes.com (February 5, 2013). https://www.forbes.com/sites/melaniehaiken/2013/02/05/22-the-number-of-veterans-who-now-commit-suicide-every-day/?sh=346d761e2e97.

Jameson Hunter Ltd. "Sailing Trim" Image (2021). http://elizabethqueen-seaswann.com/Business_Plan/Sailing_Trim_Tacking_Beating_Beam_Weather_Broad_Reach.html.

Joint Training Division (Joint Staff J7). Joint Officers Handbook (JOH) Staffing and Action Guide, 3rd Edition, 2012.

Kamen, Robert Mark, James Lineberger, and Darryl Ponicsan. *Taps* (film based on the novel *Father Sky* by Devery Freeman). Los Angeles: 20th Century Fox, 1981. http://tutor1.net/wikiquote/17252.

Lakein, Alan. *The Time of Your Life* (film based on the book *How to Get Control of Your Time and Your Life* by Alan Lakein), Hollywood, CA: The Cally Curtis Company, 1984.

Lewis, C. S. *Mere Christianity*. New York: Macmillan Publishing Co., 1952.

Live Journal. "Officers Insignia of the Armed Forces of the United States," Image. https://ateamcanon.livejournal.com/5254.html.

Price, Cadet First Lieutenant Arthur Preston '43. Alma Mater, The Citadel—The Military College of South Carolina (1943).

Lovelace, Alexander, G. "'Slap Heard around the World': George Patton and Shell Shock," *The US Army War College Quarterly: Parameters* 49, no. 3 (Autumn 2019). https://press.armywarcollege.edu/cgi/viewcontent.cgi?article=2776&context=parameters.

Markunsen, Ann. "How We Lost the Peace Dividend," The American Prospect—Ideas, Politics, and Power (Dec 19, 2001). https://prospect.org/culture/books/lost-peace-dividend/.

McCarthy, W. J. Department of the Navy, "USS GEORGE WASHINGTON (CVN 73) Command History for Calendar Year 2001," (March 13, 2002). https://www.history.navy.mil/content/dam/nhhc/research/archives/command-operation-reports/ship-command-operation-reports/g/george-washington-cvn-73-iv/pdf/2001.pdf.

Ohls, Gary J. "Eastern Exit: Rescue '. . . From the Sea,'" *Naval War College Review* 61, no. 4 (Autumn 2008).

Parker, Clifford B. "Axis powers miscalculated after early advantages in World War II, Stanford scholar says," Stanford University, Stanford News (December 12, 2017). https://news.stanford.edu/2017/12/12/axis-powers-miscalculated-early-advantages-wwii-stanford-scholar-says/.

Priolo, Gary P. (webmaster). USS GUAM Naval History, NavSource Online (November 13, 2020). http://www.navsource.org/archives/10/11/1109.htm.

Stanley, Thomas J. and William B. Danko. *The Millionaire Next Door—The Surprising Secrets of America's Wealthy*. New York: MJF Books, 1996.

Stoltz, Photographer's Mate Third Class Christopher B. April 3, 2003, Mediterranean Sea. https://commons.wikimedia.org/wiki/

File:US_Navy_030403-N-9964S-023_USS_Harry_S._Truman_(CVN_75)_comes_alongside_the_Military_Sealift_Command_Oiler_USNS_John_Lenthall_(T-AO_189)_for_an_underway_replenishment_(UNREP).jpg.

Storlie, Chad. "Lessons in Appreciating Diversity in World War II," USAA, USAA Community, (September 2016). https://communities.usaa.com/t5/Going-Civilian/Lessons-in-Appreciating-Diversity-from-World-War-II/ba-p/102348.

The Citadel—The Military College of South Carolina. The Honor Code, The Honor Manual of the South Carolina Corps of Cadets 2021-2022, Charleston, SC: The Krause Center for Leadership and Ethics, 2021.

Walsh, Brian. "Support to the Hurricane Katrina Response by the Joint Force Maritime Component Commander: Reconstruction and Issues," Center for Naval Analysis, The CNA Corporation (August 2006). https://www.cna.org/CNA_files/PDF/D0013414.A4.pdf.

Wilcox, Ella Wheeler. "Solitude" Poetry Foundation (2021). https://www.poetryfoundation.org/poems/45937/solitude-56d225aad9924.

NOTES

1. Genesis 1:17–19 (NIV).
2. Thomas J. Stanley and William B. Danko, *The Millionaire Next Door—The Surprising Secrets of America's Wealthy* (New York: MJF Books, 1996), 21–23.
3. C. S. Lewis, *Mere Christianity* (New York: Macmillan Publishing Co., 1952), 108–14.
4. Pat Conroy, *The Lords of Discipline* (New York: Random House Inc., 1980), 1.
5. Cadet First Lieutenant Arthur Preston Price '43, "Alma Mater," The Citadel—The Military College of South Carolina, (1943).
6. Ella Wheeler Wilcox, "Solitude." First published in 1883 in the *New York Sun*, (Poetry Foundation, 2021), https://www.poetryfoundation.org/poems/45937/solitude-56d225aad9924.
7. The Honor Code, *The Honor Manual of the South Carolina Corps of Cadets 2021–2022* (Charleston, SC: The Krause Center for Leadership and Ethics, The Citadel—The Military College of South Carolina, 2021), 2, 18.
8. Robert Mark Kamen, James Lineberger, and Darryl Ponicsan, *Taps* (film based on the novel *Father Sky* by Devery Freeman), (Los Angeles: 20th Century Fox, 1981), http://tutor1.net/wikiquote/17252.
9. *The Time of Your Life* (film based on the book *How to Get Control of Your Time and Your Life* by Alan Lakein), (Hollywood, CA: The Cally Curtis Company, 1974). This time management short film narrated by James Whitmore is available at https://www.youtube.com/watch?v=36-JaSqOQaw.
10. Joint Training Division (Joint Staff J7), *Joint Officers Handbook (JOH) Staffing and Action Guide*, 3rd Edition, (2012), 85.
11. Joint Training Division, *JOH*, 30.
12. FFG-28 USS *Boone*, https://www.seaforces.org/usnships/ffg/FFG-28-USS-Boone.htm.

13. Gary J. Ohls, "Eastern Exit: Rescue '. . . From the Sea,'" *Naval War College Review* 61, no. 4 (Autumn 2008): 143, https://apps.dtic.mil/sti/pdfs/ADA519194.pdf.
14. Gary P. Priolo, USS *Guam* Naval History, NavSource Online (November 13, 2020), http://www.navsource.org/archives/10/11/1109.htm.
15. Live Journal, "Officers Insignia of the Armed Forces of the United States," https://ateamcanon.livejournal.com/5254.html.
16. Ann Markunsen, "How We Lost the Peace Dividend," The American Prospect—Ideas, Politics, and Power (December 19, 2001), https://prospect.org/culture/books/lost-peace-dividend/.
17. Joshua Horn, "Was Sherman a War Criminal?" Discerning History (December 16, 2014), http://discerninghistory.com/2014/12/was-sherman-a-war-criminal/.
18. Alexander, G. Lovelace, "'Slap Heard around the World': George Patton and Shell Shock," The US Army War College Quarterly: Parameters 49, no. 3 (Autumn 2019), https://press.armywarcollege.edu/cgi/viewcontent.cgi?article=2776andcontext=parameters.
19. Scott Bomboy, "Lincoln and Taney's great writ showdown," Constitution Daily, National Constitution Center, Philadelphia, PA (May 28, 2021), https://constitutioncenter.org/blog/lincoln-and-taneys-great-writ-showdown.
20. Edmund Vance Cooke, "How Did You Die," (published in 1903), Allpoetry.com, https://allpoetry.com/How-Did-You-Die-.
21. Clifford B. Parker, "Axis powers miscalculated after early advantages in World War II, Stanford scholar says," Stanford University, Stanford News, (December 12, 2017). https://news.stanford.edu/2017/12/12/axis-powers-miscalculated-early-advantages-wwii-stanford-scholar-says/
22. Chad Storlie, "Lessons in Appreciating Diversity in World War II," USAA, USAA Community, (September 2016). https://communities.usaa.com/t5/Going-Civilian/Lessons-in-Appreciating-Diversity-from-World-War-II/ba-p/102348
23. Jameson Hunter Ltd. "Sailing Trim," Image (2021), http://elizabethqueenseaswann.com/Business_Plan/Sailing_Trim_Tacking_Beating_Beam_Weather_Broad_Reach.html.
24. Department of the Navy (Office of the Chief of Naval Operations), "Report on the Collision between USS FITZGERALD (DDG 62) and Motor Vessel ACX CRYSTAL" and "Report on the Collision

between USS JOHN S MCCAIN (DDG 56) and Motor Vessel ALNIC MC," (October 23, 2017), 57, 62–66, https://s3.amazonaws.com/CHINFO/USS+Fitzgerald+and+USS+John+S+McCain+Collision+Reports.pdf.

25. Melanie Haiken, "Suicide Rate Among Vets and Active Duty Military Jumps—Now 22 a Day," Forbes.com (February 5, 2013), https://www.forbes.com/sites/melaniehaiken/2013/02/05/22-the-number-of-veterans-who-now-commit-suicide-every-day/?sh=346d761e2e97.
26. Priolo, USS *Guam* Naval History, http://www.navsource.org/archives/10/11/1109.htm.
27. Ohls, "Eastern Exit: Rescue '. . . From the Sea,'" 126–48.
28. W. J. McCarthy, Department of the Navy, "USS GEORGE WASHINGTON (CVN 73) Command History for Calendar Year 2001," (March 13, 2002), 5–6, https://www.history.navy.mil/content/dam/nhhc/research/archives/command-operation-reports/ship-command-operation-reports/g/george-washington-cvn-73-iv/pdf/2001.pdf.
29. Photographer's Mate Third Class J. Scott Campbell, September 12, 2001, New York City, https://commons.wikimedia.org/wiki/File:US_Navy_010912-N-1407C-001_USS_George_Washington_(CVN_73).jpg.
30. Brian Walsh, "Support to the Hurricane Katrina Response by the Joint Force Maritime Component Commander: Reconstruction and Issues," Center for Naval Analysis, The CNA Corporation (August 2006), 10, https://www.cna.org/CNA_files/PDF/D0013414.A4.pdf.
31. Photographer's Mate Third Class Christopher B. Stoltz, April 3, 2003, Mediterranean Sea, https://commons.wikimedia.org/wiki/File:US_Navy_030403-N-9964S-023_USS_Harry_S._Truman_(CVN_75)_comes_alongside_the_Military_Sealift_Command_Oiler_USNS_John_Lenthall_(T-AO_189)_for_an_underway_replenishment_(UNREP).jpg.